Len Taikki

THE BODY Style

The Church as described by Jesus

GAYLE D. ERWIN

* * * * *

The Body Style

Copyright © 2002

ISBN 1-56599-255-5

YAHSHUA Publishing
PO Box 219
Cathedral City, CA 92235-0219
Phone 760-321-0077
FAX 760-202-1139

Printed in the United States of America.

Paul declared that no man lives or dies to himself. Such truth resounds to my great benefit. All I do is a collection of understandings and helps gleaned from Scripture, clarified by the Holy Spirit and assisted by large groups of people. Only in Heaven will I understand just how many people have poured wisdom and servanthood into my heart.

On a lesser plane, where I see immediately, I direct understandable gratitude. Leading that list must be my wife, Ada, who remains my best editor and friend (remarkably, at the same time) and that after 45 years of marriage. My children, Gloria and Angela (along with their husbands Peter and Mark), Valerie and Clyde demonstrate the principles I teach far better than I do.

Dave and Audrey Bjur, whom God brought to me as employees but turned out to be volunteer slaves, continually improve my projects, including this book, with discernment. Dempster Evans, designer extraordinaire, with whom I have had a profitable relationship of 33 years, designed all the "Style Series" covers. Many have unknowingly helped with this book, so I trust God to reward them openly.

Regardless, the whole of my life constantly leaps for joy and explodes with gratitude. I hope it shows.

Table of Contents

This book is about Jesus,
And his followers,
And the instructions Jesus gave them,
Plus some highly opinionated comments
By the author of the book.
The book is an incomplete work.

Blueprints

Delighted to find the product at deep discount, I eagerly opened my first put-it-together-yourself furniture kit in the early 1960's. The advertised "easy construction" kit fit my carpentry skills. All the nail and screw holes were predrilled and the wood precut to fit. Halfway through the project as hole after hole failed to line up and new ones had to be made, with instructions written by the "English spoke good" school, I began to question the engineering behind the project. Finally, minus a few critical pieces, it came together and the lean was barely perceptible after a piece of wood was chucked under a corner.

Only later did I realize that this project was a visual parable of the Church as I had known it. Jesus spoke with clarity in Matthew 16 that he would build his Church, yet it seemed to me that few holes were drilled in the right place, and, not only did new ones have to be drilled, but carpenters with hammers in each hand fought over where to drill and who would hammer. I wondered if Jesus actually engineered this project.

A speaker once asked, "If you could ask Jesus any one question and know he would answer it fully, what would it be?" My mind instantly rushed, "How did you let your Church get in such condition?" The only churches I had known were conflicted churches.

When I overheard members of a pacifist church fighting over some trivia, I disgustedly resigned myself thinking, "It's all hopeless!" Certain glimmers of hope flitted through my mind occasionally but not before the pile of bad news raised Conflict Mountain to Everest height.

A friend of mine completed his seminary training, then, enjoying the strength of his training and the intensity of his commitment, took the reigns of his first pastorate—his only pastorate. In just months, they chewed him up and spat him out. Critically burned and permanently scarred, he left pastoral ministry, though not the Kingdom, to become a successful businessman.

In an attempt to be a healing influence for those who might follow in his footsteps, he undertook a study of conflicted churches. One startling piece of information gathered was that whenever denominational officials attempted to resolve conflict, the problems became worse without exception. Another boulder on Conflict Mountain.

In 1976, commissioned by an evangelistic missions organization, I traveled around the world, investigating to see if what they were doing in missions was truly what they said they were doing. The trip took me to one part of the world where a church leader in Europe told me did not have a single Christian. However, the organization I traveled for claimed 100,000 believers in that area. Who was right? I inclined toward the organization when I attended a believers' meeting of 2,000 in a tent in one city.

Expressing my admiration to the leader at their success in evangelism, I asked, "What is the greatest problem you now face with so many new believers in this truly pioneer situation?"

"We simply win these folks to Jesus, try to teach them the Bible and get them to fellowship in home groups. We do not construct buildings. Different denominations, hearing about all these new Christians have come in and herded segments off for themselves. People are constantly asking me, 'Why are we opposed to each other now? We once loved each other, but, now, we are not supposed to have anything to do with each other.'" Another boulder on the mountain.

On that same trip, in a major world city, my hosts drove me toward the hotel where I would stay. As we passed a major church whose name I knew, my host said, "We call this church, *Battle Temple*. They fight like cats and dogs with different groups suing each other." Give this one two boulders.

Every year in Jerusalem (City of Peace!), different religions fight over access to and control of certain holy sites. In a televised news segment, I heard one church leader cast his vitriol toward another by shouting, "You and your god go to hell." The pain in my heart almost masked the sound of another boulder falling into place on Conflict Mountain. Expect any study of recorded church history to leave you disillusioned.

In spite of songs describing or calling for our unity, I found few visible examples to give me hope. I wondered if perhaps we misunderstood what Jesus meant about his building his Church. Then, like a small cry of "Help!" that drives workers to fever pitch in earthquake rubble, I heard the gentle whisper of the Creator in my heart restoring hope and eternally setting my fervor. What did I hear?

"What you see is not what I built. It is what you built. The very fact that what you build is still in existence is proof that what I am building is so strong that it even supports your vanity."

I was on my way to fresh understanding and wonderful insights.

Starting Over

If my efforts have failed so completely, only one option remains—start over. What foundation underlies the Church? Where do we begin?

Since Jesus founded the Church, his words must guide us. In Matthew 16:18, Jesus informs us of an unchangeable basic: *"...I will build my church...."* I want to let these words run through my mind over and over to cut a permanent groove, "I will build my Church; I will build my Church; I will build my Church."

Immediately, I am released from anxiety and the panic measures of *trying* to make a church grow. So many church growth and financial growth organizations should be renamed *desperate measures* companies. We long for success, especially as we view media-featured mega-churches, and adopt any measure that promises results.

Where do the promising measures come from? They proceed directly from the best minds the commercial and educational world can provide. Automatically we decide, "This must be the way to go—the way to success—the way to growth."

Unfortunately, we discover that man's means transferred to the church produce sparse and short-lived results. We could expect meager results if we listened to some key words of our founder and builder: *"What is highly valued among men is detestable in God's sight."* (Luke 16:15) We do well to learn that if the world can think it up, it probably isn't our method.

Many successful cultural systems are brought into the church without questioning their Kingdom value. Competition is one of them. How often contests among Christians are used to create a surge in attendance or fervor. Competition fits secular society but poisons Christian relationships. The offered prizes corrupt the contestants and demean the seekers unfortunate enough to be a body to be counted.

Those who use such methods watch their growth snap back to precontest levels and the muscle used to resist strengthened in the people. Future contests demand greater prizes and smoother manipulation to work. And then the results remain temporary.

Other methods mimic the world. Recently a form of saturation phone calling used in the commercial world reached into the church as a desperation measure to become known. Sloganeering continues as if it helps the church grow any better than it helps dictators control people. Cute themes are supposed to galvanize people to work and institutions to grow, but they don't. Where did "Save the world by 2000" get us? "Plant a church a day in 2000." Did we? How many churches closed their doors in that slogan period? About all sloganeering does is provide jobs for slogan writers.

I will build my Church rings comfortably and rings true. If God doesn't build it, expect it to crash. Since he builds it, I don't need to sweat in his presence. Indeed, he indicates that its growth comes from prayer rather than our cleverness:

Then he said to his disciples, "The harvest is plentiful but the workers are few. Ask the Lord of the harvest, therefore, to send out workers into his harvest field." (Matthew 9:37-38)

Foundation Stone

Some believe that the Church is built on Peter, the apostle. Those who build on Peter get Peter's results and continue to deny (through legalistic means) and/or defend Christ, cutting off ears in the crunch.

Simply put, Jesus never said he would build the Church on Peter. Peter was but a pebble as Jesus declared in calling him Peter, but the rock on which the Church was to be built was a massive stone—the word Jesus used for the foundation. Indeed, this massive stone was the foundation stone that the builders rejected—Jesus himself. It is noteworthy that early Christians in the first fruit of denominationalism called themselves "of Paul," "of Apollos" or "of Jesus" and not "of Peter."

Peter had just declared (by revelation, not logic) that Jesus was *the Messiah, the son of the living God.* (Matthew 16:16) That declaration and understanding is also the rock on which the Church is built.

Not only is Jesus and the recognition of his divinity the foundation of the Church, it is the quickest litmus test for those who stray into the heretical. Every cult, every heresy somehow reduces Jesus in its theology. Sometimes the reduction is most clever—a great leader, a prophet, Satan's *good* brother, etc.

Sometimes, the reduction hides under the guise of *Jesus plus.* Some additional work or sacrifice or belief is required *beyond* Jesus in order to be the *saved* in their system. Thus, Jesus is viewed as somehow inadequate and additional post-death work must be done. However done, a reduction is a reduction.

Entry Level

In case anyone attempts to bypass the clear declaration or subvert it, Jesus clarifies his status without question in John 10:8-9:

"I am the gate for the sheep. All who ever came before me were thieves and robbers, but the sheep did not listen to them. I am the gate; whoever enters through me will be saved."

Is that clear enough? The great majority of people are *climbing the walls* trying to achieve salvation of some sort. True salvation is available only by coming in the gate—Jesus.

Gates of Hell

Hell (or Hades) in the Scripture simply means the place of departed spirits. (Don't let anyone fool you into thinking there is no *hell* of punishment. *Destruction* and *weeping and wailing and gnashing of teeth* and *where the worm dieth not* is all you need for refutation of the *no hell* theology.) Thus, the *gates of Hell* simply signify death. Here, Jesus informs us that death will never defeat his Church either in eradication on earth or in deletion of rewards after physical life has ended.

To the follower of Jesus, death loses all power. Death, no longer the fearful end of things, provides instead the door to the glory of being with Christ. The greatest of all powers on this earth is the power over death. That power infuses the Church.

Keys to the Kingdom

Artists depict the keys in many ways. Humor abounds about Peter tending the gates of Heaven. Let's bring this back to earth.

Basically, Jesus is stating that the Kingdom will be built on him. He is the gate, and the declaration of his lordship unlocks that gate. He remains God's great mystery (secret), *the mystery that has been kept hidden for ages and generations, but is now disclosed to the saints.* (Colossians 1:26) Thus, he is the gate, the secret, the key placed in the hands of every believer.

This availability of the key is clearly stated by Jesus in John 3:16 when he uses the word *whosoever*. The purpose of his coming was to reveal the Father to us and the way of salvation. To keep the key, the secret, in the hands of a muddled few would negate his purpose. Welcome to the Kingdom. Here is the key!

Heaven Bound

"...whatever you bind on earth will be bound in heaven, and whatever you loose on earth will be loosed in heaven." (Matt 16:19)

In simplest terms, Jesus tells us that Heaven will cooperate with us. If we use the keys, doors will open. If we don't use the keys, doors will remain shut. In the most dramatic way, Jesus turns the effort and effect of the Kingdom and its evangelism over to us. Now, we see some of the reasons why the visible church is in its mess—we lost the keys to the Kingdom.

Further evidence is Jesus' statement, *"Neither do men pour new wine into old wineskins."* (Matthew 9:17), mirroring the keys declaration. When we shut the doors through denominational deterioration, those doors remain shut and cannot be opened. If we open new doors of belief and evangelism, growth proves the doors will remain open. Heaven cooperates.

Character

In *The Jesus Style* (Yahshua Publishing) I describe in detail the character of Jesus. Here I give a condensed version to provide the foundation for this book. In his *greatest in the Kingdom* teachings Jesus reveals his nature:

1. **He was a servant/slave**.

Jesus was the one, truly others-centered person. That becomes obvious in the Scripture, Matthew 20:28, as well as in his life of teaching and healing. No evidence exists that he ever did one selfish act.

2. **He did not *lord it over* others**.

Though he created the universe and had the power to do anything he wanted (the great temptation proved that), he refused to take advantage of anyone. All who followed him chose to follow him. He gave the apostles freedom to leave him. How powerful and freeing his statement: *"If you love me, you will obey what I command."* (John 14:15) How absolutely different from the leadership of the world: Jesus called them together and said, *"You know that the rulers of the Gentiles lord it over them, and their high officials exercise authority over them. Not so with you. Instead, whoever wants to become great among you must be your servant....* " (Matthew 20:25-26)

3. **He led by example**.

Jesus reduced his Kingdom to the simplest terms, *"Follow me."* He never expects us to do anything he has not shown us how to do. In John 13:15, after washing the disciples' feet (the lowest slave job), he uses the word, example: *"I have set you an example that you should do as I have done for you."* How different from the religious leaders of then and now: *"The teachers of the law and the Pharisees sit in Moses' seat. So you must obey them and do everything they tell you. But do not do what they do, for they do not practice what they preach. They tie up heavy loads and put them on men's shoulders, but they themselves are not willing to lift a finger to move them."* (Matthew 23:2-4)

Once again, note in Matthew 20:28, after encouraging the arguing disciples to be servant-hearted, he then says *"Just as..."* in describing his own leadership by example.

4. **He humbled himself as a child**.

After establishing the principle, *"Whosoever therefore shall humble himself as this little child, the same is greatest in the kingdom of heaven."* (Matthew 18:4 KJV), Jesus exhibited the same honesty and gentleness as a child. No deception issued from him: *...God is light, and in him is no darkness at all.* (I John 1:5 KJV) Jesus never threatened anyone physically though the religious rulers were terrified of him spiritually. The rulers wouldn't arrest him, not because they were afraid of Jesus physically, but because they were afraid of the crowd.

How totally congruous his life with the expression of his name: *I AM*.

5. **He served as the *younger*.**

(Luke 22:26 KJV) This means little to us today compared to the time of Jesus. The elder brother received the birthright (another expression foreign to us). The birthright provided the elder with authority, position, power and the majority of the inheritance. Basically, Jesus was telling us to live as pilgrims passing through, knowing that the world will be hostile to us and to avoid attachment to the things of this world. Notice that at his death, his only possession to be left was his clothing.

6. **He lived as the least and last**.

(Luke 9:48; Mark 9:35) No other leader, before or since, has so thoroughly placed us first and lived only for our benefit. No one could ever accuse him of graft. They accused him of eating with sinners, but not of taking bribes.

7. **He used no physical force on us**.

The Apostle Paul carries our understanding further in a remarkable passage: *Let this mind be in you, which was also in Christ Jesus: Who, being in the form of God, thought it not robbery to be equal with God...* (Philippians 2:5-6 KJV) In this verse, Paul describes Jesus as not forcing himself on us or the Kingdom. Confirming this idea, the prophecy of Isaiah recorded by Matthew states: *He shall not strive, nor cry; neither shall any man hear his voice in the streets. A bruised reed shall he not break, and smoking flax shall he not quench....* (Matthew 12:19-20 KJV) Matthew simply restates Jesus' gentleness.

8. **He was not driven by selfish ambition**.
The passage from Philippians 2, when analyzed, also informs us that Jesus' selflessness continued. Indeed, in the great temptation, when Satan offered him the opportunity to own the kingdoms of the world with only one price, *bow down and worship me*, Jesus made the choice that Adam and Eve failed to do and quoted the Scripture that showed the turn of his heart, *"You shall worship the Lord your God and him only you shall serve."* (Matthew 4:10 NKJ) At that moment, Jesus decided that his heavenly goal could be achieved only by heavenly methods. No blind ambition here.

9. **He made himself of no reputation**.
But made himself of no reputation, and took upon him the form of a servant, and was made in the likeness of men: (Philippians 2:7 KJV) He emptied himself and made himself of no image—no style or haughty bearing that would project himself above others. From his birthplace to his choice of disciples to his mode of death—everything collected to lower his reputation. Please note that he made himself of *no* reputation, not *bad*

reputation. For this reason, every person of every level of life could approach him comfortably. Indeed, sinners seemed to be comfortable in his presence.

10. **He was truly human**.

Centuries ago, the church fathers struggled with just who Jesus was: Was he God acting like a man? Was he man acting like a god? Was he half God and half man? Just who was he? They finally chose what I think was the correct answer: He was fully God and fully man. How can this be? How can God in all his purity and holiness be wedded to this sinful flesh? I don't know, but I like it. Now I can understand how he can be *touched by the feeling of my infirmities* (Hebrews 4:15), and how he can plead my case before the Father as my *wonderful Counselor* (Hebrews 7:25; Isaiah 9:6).

11. **He was obedient**.

(Philippians 2:8) Jesus' walk on earth wrapped flesh around the nature of God, the Father, and showed us how life works in the streets. Jesus only did what he saw the Father do and only said what he heard the Father say. Scripture informs us that God wants obedience to his word rather than sacrifice (1 Samuel 15:22).

12. **He was obedient even unto death**.

(Philippians 2:8) Nothing tests our servanthood like facing death as a consequence. In spite of all Peter and Satan did to keep him from going to the cross, Jesus remained faithful. His servanthood was complete. Lest we fear a blow to the Kingdom, we must record the next verses—the ones that establish his position in the Kingdom.

Therefore God exalted him to the highest place and gave him the name that is above every name, that at the name of Jesus every knee should bow, in heaven and on earth and under the earth, and every tongue confess that Jesus Christ is Lord, to the glory of God the Father. (Philippians 2:9-11)

The Core

From that time on Jesus began to explain to his disciples that he must go to Jerusalem and suffer many things at the hands of the elders, chief priests and teachers of the law, and that he must be killed and on the third day be raised to life. (Matthew 16:21)

Now that the revelation of Jesus as Messiah and founder of the Church had cleared the air, Jesus taught them the most difficult and most basic of Kingdom theology—his death and resurrection. To the natural mind, resurrection is ludicrous. To the natural mind, anyone with the power Jesus had should be impervious to any human opposition. Suffer? Forget it! A cross? Does not compute! A resurrection? Unbelievable!

From the natural mind standpoint, Peter, still swimming in the glory of his revelation, confronts Jesus with a rebuke: *"Never, Lord!" he said. "This shall never happen to you!"* (Matthew 16:22) This response of Peter predicts similar responses of the church of this day whose leaders lose their way by denying or just questioning the resurrection. The response of Jesus remains the same today as then: *"Get behind me, Satan! You are a stumbling block to me; you do not have in mind the things of God, but the things of men."* (Matthew 16:23)

Gouge the resurrection out of the core of the Church and watch it crumble before you. Many rebel at the resurrection because it seems so *unscientific*, so out of step with modern rationality. Okay! No claim exists that this phenomenon fits within the realm of man's best thinking. True, it may be man's best dream, but considered unattainable. However, our realm of logic slinks away humiliated when placed beside the reality of God's power. If we worship our brains, we will never see his truth. If we choose to believe, the door to phenomenal reality opens to us.

If we decide to reduce the resurrection to myth or to stories that man invents to fill some primal need, we must bear the direct consequence of our decision—lining up side by side with Satan. Any group, no matter how fancy their clothing or well-trained their clergy, who chooses to believe any less than what the Founder of the Church expresses as minimal, reduces themselves to no more than a social club. Their basis is *lack of faith*, not faith. Either the resurrection or no church!

Find Your Life

Then Jesus said to his disciples, "If anyone would come after me, he must deny himself and take up his cross and follow me. For whoever wants to save his life will lose it, but whoever loses his life for me will find it. What good will it be for a man if he gains the whole world, yet forfeits his soul? Or what can a man give in exchange for his soul?" (Matthew 16:25-26)

Here, we touch eternity. This principle glues the universe together—the atom that builds all other foundations of Scripture. This principle chisels itself on the cornerstone of every believer's heart. Here is the Church unstoppable. Here Jesus paints with even greater clarity the basis of denying ourselves.

Here, also, is the great divine oxymoron, the mutually exclusive terms that ultimately keep the Church from ever becoming a social club. If you want to find your life, lose it? Natural thinking never develops this idea. Does this mean, now that I am a Christian, shoot me? Certainly not! It means that now my life is lived for God and others rather than myself. Nothing in your natural thought teaches that—only God!

Indeed, this statement reveals the very basic nature of God himself. Clues abound in Scripture.

Look at Matthew 20:28 for instance: "...just as the Son of Man did not come to be served, but to serve, and to give his life as a ransom for many."

Unearthly Requirements

This serving statement of Jesus also reveals a highly misunderstood yet extremely straightforward requirement for the Kingdom of God—self denial. We reword this mandate by stating, "Let a man deny himself something." The addition of something makes this requirement far less than what Jesus said. Indeed, I find it easy to deny myself some thing. In fact, we easily institutionalize this practice by designating a certain time of the year to play this little game. Lent makes us feel religious but totally misses the point. While self denial may include some things, it brings me face to face with something far more serious.

The one most ungodlike, Jesus opposing trait I carry is my self centeredness. My greed and lust (characteristics of my selfish being) rule until I invite the Creator to rule my life. When he rules, my nature gradually changes to others-centered thinking. If I simply deny myself some thing, I escape without denying my self. It is precisely that lost self that Jesus came to rescue.

This brings up a most interesting aberration that exists in the church world. When governments or other counting bodies attempt to divide the world into different religious groups, Christian becomes anyone who is not Muslim or Jewish or Hindu or Buddhist. Consequently, you find countries in civil warfare as Christians versus whomever. Although many among them might actually be believers, this system is nothing more than ascribing the word Christian to a political party. Man-thought requires no self denial. Membership in a political party is not the same as membership in the Kingdom. In United States terms, Republican is not the same as Christian and Democrat is not the same as sinner. Being American or Methodist or Catholic or Baptist—make the list as long as you want—does not make me Christian. Politicians form broad lists of various groups as the Christian world, but these lists lack something most important—the category does not necessarily denote a relationship with Jesus.

Jesus made two more statements that provide foundation stones in this same sentence: *Take up your cross and follow me.* Many things, often humorous—such as husbands and halitosis—pile into this sack we call the cross. Almost anything we consider miserable from spouse to job to inescapable situations we tend to call our cross. Keep in mind that when Jesus made this statement to the disciples, he had not yet been to the cross. No such connotations existed.

When Jesus said, Take up your cross, an immediate image flooded the disciples' minds. Thousands of people had died on crosses by that time at the hands of the Romans. The hatred all Jews had for the Romans meant that each person carried the realization that, in Roman terms, he was deserving of crucifixion. The concept of the cross also carried the ultimate reality of physical death. Consequently, this cross to be carried was a constant reminder of guilt (deserved) and death (physically inescapable).

In the face of guilt (which buffaloed Freud and still does modern psychiatrists) and death, what shall you do with your life? What goals and actions become worthwhile? With a gun to your head and permission to do your last deeds, what would they be? Jesus provides the answer, *"follow me."*

That statement, follow me, wonderfully simplifies my world. Following a person is so much simpler than following directions. Many people think Christianity is following a set of rules or principles. When I hear people say, "I try to live by Christian principles," I want to jump in and say, "Principles did not die on the cross; a person did."

I can follow even when I don't understand the directions. Often, in my travels, I am in countries that use our alphabet and within a week, I have developed a traveler's understanding of signs and the language. However, I also travel to countries whose writing baffles me. The symbols look like someone with a mouth full of chocolate sneezed. How can I learn that or follow directions in such foreign scratchings? I tried once and finally gave up, calling a friend on the phone and saying, "I can't find you."

His question worsened my situation, "Where are you?"

"I don't know."

I wanted to say, "I am at the corner of 'Walk' and 'Don't Walk.'"

So he asked me what buildings I could see. When I described them, he responded, "I know where you are. Stay there. I will come and you can follow me home." *Alriiiight!* I can follow even when I don't understand the directions.

This is why even a child can be a Christian. We do not need a Ph.D. to be a follower. All we need do is focus our eyes on Jesus himself and follow. Perhaps a better term to identify a Christian is a follower of Jesus. This term, follower, keeps us from the shifts of cultural influence and focuses our eyes where they belong.

Every religion of the earth places burdens or expectations on mankind that, try as he might, overwhelms him. Each religion demands certain forms of good to be done in order to achieve some form of salvation or heaven. Often, the good reduces to strange rituals or great sacrifice. After the rituals and sacrifice, the person remains no better nor better off than before.

Modern complaints about the missionaries changing native Hawaiians away from their native religions do not consider the whole story. On a boat tour of one Hawaiian harbor, the guide pointed out a fine home on a coveted shore and identified it as the home of a grandson of a missionary. His hostile comment followed: "As you can see, they came to do good and did well." I have no idea what brought about the prosperity of this grandson (no such hostile comment would be made about a politician or a criminal) but the guide totally avoided the real story.

On another trip, my wife and I were part of a group being guided through a state park in Hawaii. The guide, a young woman, constantly threw barbs at Christians for how they had changed the customs of the Islanders. As she told the story of old Hawaiian kings being buried in a secret place by a close associate who would return to the village and make a sacrifice, I could no longer hold back.

I asked, "What kind of sacrifice would he make?"

Her answer: "A significant sacrifice."

"Okay," I pursued, "Just how significant a sacrifice?"

"Well, a human sacrifice," she admitted.

I pressed further: "What kind of human sacrifice?"

Again, she was forced to admit something she would never normally tell those she guided, "Often, the one who buried the king would return and kill all the king's friends and family."

That was all I needed. "Do you realize that this human sacrifice would continue today were it not for the missionaries? Do you realize that you might have been killed by now even as a young lady? Do you also realize that in their culture, you, as a woman, would never be permitted to guide such a group as ours today? Be thankful the missionaries came. Be thankful." Speechless now, she only nodded reluctant agreement toward the truth.

Jesus came, not to mess up our lives as the park guide wanted us to believe, but to give us life and more of it than we ever imagined. The problem to the natural me is that the only way to achieve that life (and joy and happiness) is through giving life to others. Ironically, I achieve more happiness, simply as a fringe benefit, than others receive through my gift.

What a price people pay when they follow some path other than Jesus himself. On a recent trip to Nepal, I discovered a most interesting revelation about Buddhism. Buddhists of today, though they revere Buddha and build multitudes of statues of him, have thoroughly rejected his teachings even using almost obscene words to describe his way compared to modern Buddhism with its sacred use of sex and drugs. So long denial, hello flesh!

The wonder of following Jesus is that more is demanded of us than of any other system, yet we are the only ones whose leader occupies us and actually meets the unmeetable requirements in us. Any other teaching is a reduction of the words of Jesus.

Heaven on Earth

The promise of finding our lives carries a greater message than we usually understand. This is the promise of achieving what all people seek. Everyone wants to improve his life, to find some place of satisfaction, some happiness, some rest. An English poet named Pope described the human situation: "Hope springs eternal in the human breast. Man never is, but always to be, blessed." The constant hunt for life goes on. Even the founders of the United States recognized the reach was beyond our grasp when they declared that we all have the right to "life, liberty and the pursuit of happiness." Such wisdom they showed by knowing that happiness in the natural or political realm was only a pursuit.

However, he who made us knows how we work. Whenever you take a car or truck to a mechanic to have him tune it up, you want to make sure that he has a manufacturer's manual so he will have the right specifications. If the mechanic looks at your car and says, "Wow, I have never seen one of these before. Just leave it here and I will play with it," you will be out of there like lightning.

To our great benefit, he who made us, our manufacturer, wrote a manufacturer's manual, the Bible, so we would have the specifications to truly run right, to find our lives and not be at the mercy of arbitrary soul mechanics. We were not designed by the creator for selfishness, for wickedness, but, instead, for servanthood and holiness. Any other use of ourselves than servanthood is like sand in place of oil in the engine—we are destined for destruction, running poorly and temporarily in the meantime.

Years ago, I happened upon a journal of psychology which reported the results of a study of happiness. Now, happiness is hard to study. You cannot quantify it—put numbers on it. You cannot say, "I would like a pound of happiness, please," or, "Could I have $5.00 worth of happiness?" A group of psychologists performed the study in a way I thought was very clever. They interviewed a large number of people and asked them if they knew anyone who was happy. If they said, "Yes," there were additional questions, some standardized and others to free them to describe. After gathering a statistically significant number, they began to tabulate the data and discovered that one trait seemed to be true of all happy people—they were constantly doing benevolent things for other people.

I could have saved them a lot of time and trouble with the words of Jesus, *"If you want to find your life, lose it for me."* This is what the Kingdom, the Church, the Life is all about. This is the foundation, the stone that keeps us unmovable. Anything else is sand.

In the Name of the Lord

A s Jesus lived out the methods of and gave directions for the Church he founded, he made a statement that resulted in much opposition from his hearers. His source was clear and direct:

"I tell you the truth, the Son can do nothing by himself; he can do only what he sees his Father doing, because whatever the Father does the Son also does." (John 5:19)

"For I did not speak of my own accord, but the Father who sent me commanded me what to say and how to say it.... So whatever I say is just what the Father has told me to say." (John 12:49-50)

So, Jesus did not come to develop something different from what God, the Father, had said before nor to destroy his earlier works. The teachers of the law had done a thorough job of doing things differently. Instead, Jesus came to show us exactly what the Father was like and what he had in mind. Jesus took the very nature of the Father, stretched skin around it, and lived it out for us.

Here is the nature he heard and lived:

1. Compassionate
2. Gracious
3. Slow to anger
4. Abounding in mercy
5. Abounding in faithfulness
6. Mercy to thousands
7. Forgiving wickedness
8. Forgiving rebellion
9. Forgiving sin
10. Vengeance on those who hate him
(Exodus 34:6-7)

Jesus declared that the Holy Spirit would be along side us and in us and just like himself. The Spirit works to accomplish worldwide what Jesus exampled in a very small country but in a very big way. So thoroughly did Jesus obey the Father, it is little wonder that we call the following scene the *Triumphant Entry.*

They took palm branches and went out to meet him, shouting, "Hosanna!" "Blessed is he who comes in the name of the Lord!" "Blessed is the King of Israel!" (John 12:13)

When the crowd gathered on that day we call Palm Sunday, they shouted certain statements to Jesus that held great meaning. The first word, *Hosanna*, recognized that he was the source of salvation. Basically it means, *save us* or *save now*. Understood, though not spoken because of the prohibitions of religious leaders, was the word *Yahweh*, the name God chose for himself. So, the crowd was actually shouting, "Yahweh, save us." Riding on the donkey was the answer, *Yahshua*, the actual name of Jesus. That name means, *Yahweh saves*. What an incredible moment of recognition just prior to another shout, *"Crucify Him!"* They recognized Jesus for who he was—God incarnate, in the flesh, touchable, merciful.

The shouting continued: *"Blessed is he who comes in the name of the Lord!"* A mountain of meaning infuses that cry. Today, names have minimal meaning. We look for names in baby books, names that sound good; and we play a little with spelling for individuality. Meaning is secondary. However, back in biblical days, names always carried meaning. In the oldest time, people were named in accordance with who they were. Thus, if you knew a person's name and the meaning of the name, you knew the person.

So, what might have been in the minds of the crowd with such a declaration? Perhaps they remembered Exodus 34:6 where God defined his name to Moses. Perhaps they walked through each trait of God's name and recognized that each trait perfectly described Jesus and that he had truly come in *the Name of the Lord*.

Now, if this is true of God, the Father, and also true of Jesus, when he used the term *in my name*, it takes on great significance. Whatever done in his name must match the list above or it is not in his name. Simple enough. But what benefits and responsibilities await us *in his name?*

Welcoming children – Matthew 18:5
Fellowship – Matthew 18:20
Rewards from a cup of water – Mark 9:41
Spiritual power – Mark 16:17
Prayer – John 14:13-14
Presence of the Holy Spirit – John 14:26

So, members of the Church being built by Jesus go (as he did) obediently and powerfully *in his name* and what a name it is!

Access to God

In keeping with the cry of any human heart, the disciples observed the access Jesus had to God, the Father, and longed for it enough to ask, *Lord, teach us to pray, just as John taught his disciples.* (Luke 11:1) Though they remained a rag-tag group not observably capable of handling such power, Jesus, without hesitation, taught them. Even their manipulative method of comparing to John did not deter the teaching.

Immediately, this informs me that Jesus practiced what he preached. He did his praying in private which is why they had to ask and could not analyze the prayer to develop their own. This also informs me that Jesus is far more interested in our access to God than even we are.

As he prepares to teach them, he makes sure they understand that prayer is not for show or for mindless repetition but for true communication with God. So, he taught them:

"After this manner therefore pray ye: Our Father which art in heaven, Hallowed be thy name. Thy kingdom come. Thy will be done in earth, as it is in heaven. Give us this day our daily bread. And forgive us our debts, as we forgive our debtors. And lead us not into temptation, but deliver us from evil:

For thine is the kingdom, and the power, and the glory, for ever. Amen." (Matthew 6:9-13 KJV)

Our Father in Heaven

What incredible access. We can call God "Dad." It is almost as if nothing else need be said. If God is our Dad, what do we lack? But this also means God is willing to call us his child. Awesome. This certainly shows how wide his arms extend—even to those whose behavior sometimes violates their spiritual heritage.

Hallowed be thy name

Name meant much more than a collection of letters. Names had meanings then. To know a person's name and the meaning of the name was to know the person. How different from our day. Remember that God defines his name to Moses in Exodus 34:6 as being: *"compassionate, gracious, slow to anger, abounding in mercy and faithfulness, mercy to thousands, forgiving wickedness, forgiving rebellion, forgiving sin."*

How exciting and fulfilling to honor him for these traits and glorify him for the evidence we see of his action in our behalf. When we take the time to do this, the next step becomes self-evident:

Thy kingdom come

Here the prayer becomes very personal. "I want you to be king of me, to dominate me, to be in charge of my life, to call the shots in my life." When we know what he is like and honor him for being so good, we certainly want God to be in charge. The other options are unacceptable.

Thy will be done in earth as it is in heaven

Once we have declared God to be our Dad, honored him for who he is and asked him to dominate us, we are in better position to pray with more wisdom and discernment for his will. John makes it clear:

This is the confidence we have in approaching God: that if we ask anything according to his will, he hears us. And if we know that he hears us—whatever we ask—we know that we have what we asked of him. (1 John 5:14-15)

Having this knowledge and relationship unlocks the miraculous in our prayer, since we are in better position to know what his will might be.

Give us this day our daily bread

Well, at least we know he wants to hear from us every day, such is his love for us. I tend to want to pray for next year's bread today so I won't have to be such a bother to God. Ah, but he prefers to be bothered. He also knows that if he gave me next year's bread today, I would eat it today.

Most of all, this part of the prayer speaks of needing our daily supply of the *bread of life* which is Jesus.

And forgive us our debts, as we forgive our debtors

Jesus presupposes our fallibility, accepts the reality of our weakness and assures us of forgiveness. God's kids can sleep the sweet sleep of peace because of his forgiveness. This part of the prayer attaches something new for the disciples to consider, *as we forgive our debtors*. Prior to this teaching by Jesus, no clear theology existed requiring forgiveness of others. Indeed, Jesus confronted the *eye for an eye and tooth for a tooth* thinking of the populace.

Now, our forgiveness demands that we forgive others. Knowing this idea would stagger the apostles, Jesus carefully commented, *"For if ye forgive men their trespasses, your heavenly Father will also forgive you: But if ye forgive not men their trespasses, neither will your Father forgive your trespasses."* (Matthew 6:14) Logic certainly calls us, if we have honored God for being forgiving and then asking him to dominate us, to follow with being forgiving..

Jesus knew that forgiveness provides freedom and saves us from being tortured. He makes that very clear when Peter brings the subject up again in Matthew 18 wanting to know how often he should forgive his brother. In the illustration that followed, lack of forgiveness subjected the unforgiving servant to the *torturers.* The servant had been forgiven a massive debt, yet he couldn't forgive a very small debt owed to him. Often people defend their unforgiveness to me by saying, "You don't realize what they did to me." The simple answer is, we don't realize how much we did to God. We have been forgiven a massive amount. People on this earth have the power to do very little to us compared to how much we have done to God.

Lead us not into temptation

Keep us ahead of the game of life. We know our weaknesses and sources of temptation. Here, we pray that God will enable us to deal with these weaknesses ahead of time and not have to wrestle with them in a testing time.

Deliver us from evil

Don't let us do anything that will detrimentally affect this wonderful relationship we have with you (God) or damage in any way the ministry you (God) have given to each of us.

Thine is the kingdom, and the power, and the glory, for ever.

When Satan tempted Jesus in what we call the *great temptation,* these were the three areas of temptation—the kingdom, the power and the glory. How appropriate! If there is anything we humans long for and ardently seek, it is kingdom, power and glory. Knowing that these hang ever before our eyes, we need to daily place them in God's corner and at his feet. Whew! Truly daily!

Amen

Sealed and certain. Finished and in no need of reconsideration. Prayer of the highest order.

However, even with such clear presentation of access to God, Jesus knew that the disciples were *very sloooow learners.* Have you noticed how often Jesus repeated himself in the Gospels? There was a reason. So, he gives additional illustration in Luke 11:5-8 of certain access:

Then he said to them, "Suppose one of you has a friend, and he goes to him at midnight and says, 'Friend, lend me three loaves of bread, because a friend of mine on a journey has come to me, and I have nothing to set before him.' Then the one inside answers, 'Don't bother me. The door is already locked, and my children are with me in bed. I can't get up and give you anything.' I tell you, though he will not get up and give him the bread because he is his friend, yet because of the man's boldness he will get up and give him as much as he needs."

At first read, this seems to show a resistant God, however it is the exact opposite. Hospitality in a Mideast village is the highest morality and highest honor a person can have. Not to be able to offer hospitality/bread drove this man at midnight (no stores open) to his neighbor. Hospitality in these villages was the responsibility of the whole village; so this man, when he came at midnight, knew that his neighbor knew the village rules. He knew that he would get the bread. It was a foregone conclusion.

Only one question remained, "Why do you want the bread?" Had he desired to simply have a midnight snack, he would have returned unfulfilled; however, he wanted to bless someone else and lacked the means to do so. Note that he leaves with "*as much as he needs.*" Amazing how this desire to bless others matches the servant heart of Jesus.

So, Jesus is giving a strong illustration of absolute access to God. He is saying that Heaven feels your inadequacies and is on your side. However, Jesus knew that the disciples were *very sloooow learners*, so he needed to ratchet the intensity up a notch with another illustration:

"So I say to you: Ask and it will be given to you; seek and you will find; knock and the door will be opened to you. For everyone who asks receives; he who seeks finds; and to him who knocks, the door will be opened." (Luke 11:9-10)

Jesus paints himself into a corner here by guaranteeing access to God to "*everyone who asks.*" No steps to perform, no persons to appease, no traditions to fulfill, no emotions to pump, no walls to climb.

This happens to be one of the most misunderstood verses in the Bible. Often, people say some form of this, "Let's see. I have always wanted that luxury boat. If I ask, God must give it to me." This verse is not about things, it is about access to God. Why would God ruin you with something that will burn?

However, Jesus knew that the disciples were *very slooow learners* and three very clear illustrations would not suffice, so again he approaches the subject but now from a different angle:

"Which of you fathers, if your son asks for a fish, will give him a snake instead? Or if he asks for an egg, will give him a scorpion? If you then, though you are evil, know how to give good gifts to your children, how much more will your Father in heaven give the Holy Spirit to those who ask him!" *(Luke 11:11-13)*

Aha! Our great and generous Heavenly Father gives us the very best—himself, the Holy Spirit. Disappointed that it wasn't a boat? God knows that *things* will never meet our inadequacies nor will they cause us to be *others-centered* and enable us to give ourselves away. And all we have to do is ask! God limits himself to our asking. He will not violate us or force himself on us. We must ask. But then, it is a foregone conclusion. No traditions, no exclusions, no embarrassments, no lies, no hesitancies. We individually have automatic, ultimate access to our God if we wish. No strings attached except to our desire.

Many hold to the belief that God looks for and blesses *sweet people*. If you have been a *sweet person* all your life, then God must bless you, or when they bury you, certainly God must welcome you. God would love to bless *sweet people*, if he could find any, but he simply can't. So he has to bless us! Am I grateful! What a Church!

Justice, Mercy, Faith

"Woe to you, teachers of the law and Pharisees, you hypocrites! You give a tenth of your spices—mint, dill and cummin. But you have neglected the more important matters of the law—justice, mercy and faithfulness. You should have practiced the latter, without neglecting the former. You blind guides! You strain out a gnat but swallow a camel." (Matthew 23:24)

This must be one of the most humorous statements in Scripture. Try and visualize it without laughing. You can't. Surely Jesus illustrated the ridiculousness of the Pharisaical position in the gnat/camel statement. They were so careful with little things, so very careful.

However, the very nature of legalism forces you to think about yourself and how well *you* are doing. Also, the very nature of legalism proves that we cannot keep the law. We are unable to write a law that we can keep. Indeed, the law of the Old Testament was given to us to prove that we cannot keep God's Law. Through the centuries, the religious leaders added additional commentary that became as important as the Law itself, but along with the commentary came ways of escape, sometimes quite silly.

The Pharisees and other religious leaders carefully measured out the tithe on minutia to cover their own tracks while showing complete disregard for the masses whom they considered inferior and cursed of God. In response to an appropriate question, Jesus condensed the entire question of life to two commandments:

Hearing that Jesus had silenced the Sadducees, the Pharisees got together. One of them, an expert in the law, tested him with this question: "Teacher, which is the greatest commandment in the Law?"

Jesus replied: "'Love the Lord your God with all your heart and with all your soul and with all your mind.' This is the first and greatest commandment. And the second is like it: 'Love your neighbor as yourself.' All the Law and the Prophets hang on these two commandments." (Matthew 12:34-40)

Did you notice verse 40? The entire Law and Prophets (in other words—the Bible) hang on love of God and others. Nowhere did the legalists and do the legalists fail more. Bluntly put, legalism breeds and feeds on self-centeredness.

In the sharpest of contrasts, where Jesus rules, justice, mercy and faith—all traits that center on others outside of ourselves—provide our foundation. Trying to *live right* revolves around how we treat others rather than how well we are doing personally. In the greatest of joyous ironies, when we treat others properly, we are, indeed, doing right personally.

In John, Chapter 21, Peter and a few others of the apostolic gang were caught returning to their old pursuits. Jesus did not urge a hesitant Peter under intense questioning, *"Do you love me?"* to go and pursue inner healing or stare at his navel until he had his act together. No, he merely urged him to concentrate on giving his life away for the benefit of others, *"Feed my sheep."*

When one's life overflows with justice, mercy and faith, you never need ask if he is living right. Indeed, that person has tapped the heart of Jesus and exampled the citizen of the kingdom.

Freely, Freely

In the same mold of justice, mercy and faith, generosity shouts at us as a trait of the Kingdom exampled by Jesus. Again, generosity is definitely an *others-centered* trait. When Jesus spoke of one with *good eyes* as opposed to *evil eyes*, he spoke a common statement easily understood by the Apostles. Someone with *good eyes* was a person of generosity. *Evil eyes* meant stinginess. Note the results:

"Your eye is the lamp of your body. When your eyes are good, your whole body also is full of light. But when they are bad, your body also is full of darkness." (Luke 11:34)

Further, this passage straddles a financial commentary by Jesus which ends with the statement:

"No one can serve two masters. Either he will hate the one and love the other, or he will be devoted to the one and despise the other. You cannot serve both God and Money." (Matthew 6:24)

On the whole subject of finances (greed?) Jesus taught explicitly. One misses this only with great effort. Even before he condensed his statement in

Matthew 6:24, Jesus swam against the current of that age and ours:

"Do not store up for yourselves treasures on earth, where moth and rust destroy, and where thieves break in and steal. But store up for yourselves treasures in heaven, where moth and rust do not destroy, and where thieves do not break in and steal. For where your treasure is, there your heart will be also." (Matthew 6:19-21)

Greed stores its gains on earth; generosity stores in heaven. It doesn't get any simpler than that. However, we have further statements by and about Jesus that enlighten us more. The most famous of all single verses sets the underlying foundation of the Kingdom:

"For God so loved the world that He gave His only begotten Son, that whoever believes in Him should not perish but have everlasting life." (John 3:16 NKJ)

How clear that word *gave* makes this Scripture. God himself invented generosity. But wait, there's more! The theme of giving continues in the life of Jesus. His constitutional statement makes it clear:

"For even the Son of Man did not come to be served, but to serve, and to give his life as a ransom for many." (Mark 10:45)

Give, give, give! We hear it over and over when it comes to the heart of God. His generosity to us so exceeds the best we can do that no calculator or computer can tally:

"If you, then, though you are evil, know how to give good gifts to your children, how much more will your Father in heaven give good gifts to those who ask him!" (Matthew 7:11)

Then, in response to a worker who received the contracted pay (good pay, I might say) and complained that a worker with only a few minutes on the job received, without a contract, the same amount, Jesus said:

"Take your pay and go. I want to give the man who was hired last the same as I gave you. Don't I have the right to do what I want with my own money? Or are you envious because I am generous?" (Matthew 20:14-15)

But, as members of his Kingdom, his Church, and because we have him living in us, we naturally accrue the traits of the King. Consequently, the expectations are real:

"Heal the sick, raise the dead, cleanse those who have leprosy, drive out demons. Freely you have received, freely give." (Matthew 10:8)

Also, a little noted item occurred in the temple as funds were being brought in and deposited as offerings. With flair, those of *means* brought their offering. With shame, a widow deposited a mite, the smallest and least valued of coins but it happened to be all she had. Jesus declared that she gave more than anyone.

In that light, how informing that in 2000 AD, according to government statistics, the poorest state in the United States was the most generous in contributions to charity and church. Further light: the Christian underpinnings of the United States generate great—no, massive—generosity in this country. We are the most charitable of nations. It even pays to be defeated by us in a war because of what we contribute to rebuild the defeated. I am convinced that this is an unheralded secret of our greatness as a country.

As a final observation in this area and also as an observation of a lifetime of being a *church kid*, I believe the Kingdom is supported by poor people and not by the rich.

If the rich young ruler of Jesus' day were to come to the church today, we would have an annuity contract in front of him with blinding speed. How different the Kingdom. We look for opportunities for *outgo*! You could call our common fundraising systems, "building bigger barns." Jesus spoke direct words to a bigger-barn-raiser in Luke 12:16-21 (NLT):

And he gave an illustration: "A rich man had a fertile farm that produced fine crops. In fact, his barns were full to overflowing. So he said, 'I know! I'll tear down my barns and build bigger ones.

Then I'll have room enough to store everything. And I'll sit back and say to myself, My friend, you have enough stored away for years to come. Now take it easy! Eat, drink, and be merry!' But God said to him, 'You fool! You will die this very night. Then who will get it all?' Yes, a person is a fool to store up earthly wealth but not have a rich relationship with God."

Worship

On coming to the house, they saw the child with his mother Mary, and they bowed down and worshiped him. Then they opened their treasures and presented him with gifts of gold and of incense and of myrrh. (Matthew 2:10-11)

Some of the Pharisees in the crowd said to Jesus, "Teacher, rebuke your disciples!"
"I tell you," he replied, "if they keep quiet, the stones will cry out." (Luke 19:39-40)

"Go to the village ahead of you, and at once you will find a donkey tied there, with her colt by her. Untie them and bring them to me. If anyone says anything to you, tell him that the Lord needs them, and he will send them right away."
This took place to fulfill what was spoken through the prophet: "Say to the Daughter of Zion, 'See, your king comes to you, gentle and riding on a donkey, on a colt, the foal of a donkey.'"
The disciples went and did as Jesus had instructed them. They brought the donkey and the colt, placed their cloaks on them, and Jesus sat on them.
A very large crowd spread their cloaks on the road, while others cut branches from the trees and spread them on the road. The crowds that went

ahead of him and those that followed shouted, "Hosanna to the Son of David!" "Blessed is he who comes in the name of the Lord!" "Hosanna in the highest!"

When Jesus entered Jerusalem, the whole city was stirred and asked, "Who is this?" The crowds answered, "This is Jesus, the prophet from Nazareth in Galilee."

...But when the chief priests and the teachers of the law saw the wonderful things he did and the children shouting in the temple area, "Hosanna to the Son of David," they were indignant. "Do you hear what these children are saying?" they asked him. "Yes," replied Jesus, "have you never read, 'From the lips of children and infants you have ordained praise'?" (Matthew 21:3-16)

Jesus declared, "Believe me, woman, a time is coming when you will worship the Father neither on this mountain nor in Jerusalem. You Samaritans worship what you do not know; we worship what we do know, for salvation is from the Jews. Yet a time is coming and has now come when the true worshipers will worship the Father in spirit and truth, for they are the kind of worshipers the Father seeks. God is spirit, and his worshipers must worship in spirit and in truth."
(John 4:21-24)

Very little needs to be added. The Church Jesus is building is a worshiping church. Simply, intimately, directly worshiping. No place or emotional mood is needed. No environment required.

A rock can worship wherever it plunks down if we refuse to do so. One is no better off copying Old Testament forms that demand a certain approach to the *Holy of Holies* as if the veil still existed. Indeed, the simpler the worship and the less the distractions, the better.

The wise men sought nothing for themselves except to see and worship the creator. Wise men still seek him and still give him gifts. Children still sing of his greatness with robust and natural volume. True shepherds still noise his praise abroad. Women still speak of his authority. Men still bow to his kingship. Artists still honor his presence. Leaders still seek his guidance. His church stands in awe.

One fascinating truth develops in worship. Whenever we worship, we are truly getting out of ourselves and focusing on another. This is, of course, the core of the nature of Jesus—others. Thus, worship is great practice for the life of the Church and the believer.

Power

The daunting task of imitating Jesus left the disciples trembling in their boots. Their discomfort shows in nervous questions and final arguments in John 13-16: "We don't know the way." "Show us the Father." "Why us?" Perhaps, the apostles discerned that things were winding down, thus we understand the desperate last arguments over who was the greatest. Perhaps we see why Peter's expressed commitment to faithfulness only revealed his destiny—repeated denials of Jesus. These difficult and confusing thoughts coursed through their souls.

All hope flees at such times, except for the promise. Ah, the promise! *"I will not leave you comfortless."* No abandonment in his Church. No orphans from his presence. No overpowered weaklings. His Church was designed to have his presence genetically built in through the Holy Spirit as surely as if Jesus had never left. *"I am going to send you what my Father has promised; but stay in the city until you have been clothed with power from on high."* (Luke 24:49)

With little understanding they waited. What would be happening? How would they know? What effects would they show? His final promise helped to clarify the task. His Church would be a progressive and aggressive Church, not content to gloat over achievements and polish its awards.

No, this was to be a Church on the move, on the share, on the give, on the save. *"But you will receive power when the Holy Spirit comes on you; and you will be my witnesses in Jerusalem, and in all Judea and Samaria, and to the ends of the earth."* (Acts 1:8)

To represent Jesus (witness) properly demands far more than my nature delivers. Jesus knew that, so he promised supernatural assistance. Without it, we fail. Any church that ignores or distances the Holy Spirit strips themselves naked and shamefully deserves the taunts of the world. Any church that asks for the Holy Spirit to fill them, discovers that he works miraculously beyond themselves as if Jesus himself were there. Hmmm.

Jesus does not, as Paul does, list the giftings of the Holy Spirit. No need to if we understand that his infilling assists us in being like Jesus. Enough!

One could even say that any uses of what we might consider to be spiritual gifts that do not represent Jesus and do what he would do would be a misunderstanding and, worse, a misrepresenting. Any gift or application of a gift that does not survive an examination through the Nature of Jesus should not be permitted to continue without judgment.

What a great promise to be clothed with the power to be representatives of Jesus! And what great opportunity, as we saw in the chapter, "Access to God," that we are promised his Holy Spirit simply for the asking.

With that promise, we should never hesitate to pray for the sick or to tell demons to leave, a power delegated to us by Jesus. When we pray for the sick, the healing remains in the hands of God. We are merely to obey. When we tell a demon to leave, he has no alternative but to obey. Any actions of a person after that are the product of habit, not the effect of demons.

So, the power is present for whatever the need. Sad, that in this day, some would have a form of Godliness but deny the power.

Salt

With his story about salt, Jesus forever placed the Church in a unique position. Chemistry students know that *salts* covers a wide range of chemical substances that tend to be stable and somewhat unreactive rather than volatile.

However, table salt is only one substance, sodium chloride. Separated, sodium chloride becomes sodium and chlorine, each volatile and deadly. Together and stable, we cannot survive without it. Salt is well known for its preservative and taste-enhancing properties.

The question: How can salt lose its *savor* or saltiness? Jesus said it could and when it did, it was worthless except for added pavement. Listen to his words:

"You are the salt of the earth. But if the salt loses its saltiness, how can it be made salty again? It is no longer good for anything, except to be thrown out and trampled by men." (Matthew 5:13)

"Salt is good, but if it loses its saltiness, how can you make it salty again? Have salt in yourselves, and be at peace with each other." (Mark 9:50)

If basic chemistry carries any value in interpreting this lesson, salt loses its savor or saltiness in only two ways. The most direct and thorough way is for it to have an internal change—one that will still, perhaps, leave it in the classification of salts but changes it away from the tasty and highly usable table category. In any field but chemistry, such a change makes it useless.

In a dramatic illustration for those who live in cold climates, change the sodium to calcium (internal change) and it simply is used to throw out and be trodden under foot to give traction on ice or snow.

The second way that salt loses its savor is to become filled or adulterated with so many impurities that even the preservative qualities of salt are unable to protect from possible toxicity. The application of these two means of saltiness-loss are so obvious.

Should we choose to lose our internal and relational connection to Jesus, we no longer preserve; we poison. We no longer enhance taste; we destroy flavor. Spew! Should we let the ways and thoughts of the world pollute us, we are viewed as environmental disasters who offered hope but only provide pavement. Jesus builds a pure but highly useful church.

Light

"You are the light of the world. A city on a hill cannot be hidden. Neither do people light a lamp and put it under a bowl. Instead they put it on its stand, and it gives light to everyone in the house. In the same way, let your light shine before men, that they may see your good deeds and praise your Father in heaven." (Matthew 5:14-16)

Darkness describes many things negative to us—evil, ignorance, fear, lawlessness, backwardness, hiddenness, discouragement—the list could go on and on. The fact remains that humanity walks in darkness. Read all the great literature—it reveals the hopeless shame and evil of mankind. Listen to the songs—love hoped for but disappointed. Study the history—filled with wars and unspeakably evil leaders. When we establish heroes, someone comes along and destroys them with truth about their lives. Darkness.

Political movements and psychological theories spring up offering utopia, then fade with their failures back into darkness. Fame and riches hold out their hands, removing them at the last second and laughing us to scorn. Religions invite us to hope, then fill us with hatred and bondage. Darkness. What is it about following Jesus that makes

us the light of the world? More than most followers can describe.

First, he deletes our guilt by his death and resurrection, cleansing and forgiving.

Second, the requirements of holiness, which
none of us can meet, are provided by his strength
and Spirit in us.

Third, his presence creates a cycle of growth,
awesome and unexplainable.

Fourth, he fills us with love for others far beyond the best benevolence we could invent.

Fifth, he provides us with fellowship and family
wherever we go in the world.

Sixth, he sets us at ease about our future with
the knowledge that he watches over us and provides for us.

Seventh, we have the promise from him that we
will see him again.

Eighth, death has lost its sting and fury. The
list can go on and on.

Indeed, all the hopes and dreams of mankind
find fulfillment in Jesus. While it is true that
church history causes us to hang our heads, we
must note that the blame does not rest with Jesus. The shame arrives with corruption of the
teachings of Jesus through politics, militarism or
economics. No one could read this book, for instance, but especially no one could read the Gospels and launch a medieval crusade or genocide
or claim a *divine right* to lord it over others. These
are all corruptions.

The wonderful news is that the light (*Hooray!*)
exposes all that corruption. Jesus informs us that

men love darkness only for one reason, because their deeds are evil. Light causes the cockroaches of evil men and their plans to scurry back to their putrid lairs. Any politician who campaigns on the platform of Christianity and then hides his dealings past or present has retreated into darkness and only for one reason—evil. Any churchman who deals in secret meetings or hides the reality of his own heart has retreated into darkness and only for one reason—evil.

Jesus is unrelenting light. We need never stumble. We, as the Church, reflect that light bringing hope that will never disappoint.

Communion

And he said to them, "I have eagerly desired to eat this Passover with you before I suffer. For I tell you, I will not eat it again until it finds fulfillment in the kingdom of God." After taking the cup, he gave thanks and said, "Take this and divide it among you. For I tell you I will not drink again of the fruit of the vine until the kingdom of God comes." And he took bread, gave thanks and broke it, and gave it to them, saying, "This is my body given for you; do this in remembrance of me." In the same way, after the supper he took the cup, saying, "This cup is the new covenant in my blood, which is poured out for you." (Luke 22:15-20)

H ope and grace flow in this act we call *communion*. Hope comes because the Holy Spirit is involved in pointing us to Jesus and helping us live right. Grace flows as we attach ourselves to his goodness. Let's see if we can take some positions on the grace side of the fence.

First, many traditions exceed the authority of the Bible, thus victims of tradition abound. When Jesus began communion, his only commands were to do it and to remember him. Some groups punish people by refusing to offer communion to them; however, it should not be refused to anyone who wants to remember Jesus. Never forget how

Jesus treated Judas! Jesus shared the cup with Judas just before Judas betrayed him.

Some churches limit administration of communion to special authorities or to special buildings. Jesus placed no such limitation. The Lord's Table belongs to the people, not to the elite. Communion is for anyone who wants to remember and honor Jesus. The very life and action of Jesus proved that. This is why *common people* heard him gladly.

Second, the very act of participating in communion identifies you with the Kingdom of God and symbolizes the continuing forgiveness of sin that Jesus offers. If in your heart you want to be his and are sorry for your own sins and wish to be cleansed of them, you have every reason to want to partake of The Lord's Table. Communion reminds you that Jesus accepts you and *keeps on forgiving.*

Third, it is a celebration of what Jesus has already done, not what we have or are doing. That fact is the joy of the New Testament. Righteousness is beyond our achievement, so Jesus provided it for us by his death and resurrection. Now, all we have to do is believe on him, accept his grace and we are *in.* This calls for a party! Yes, we call the party, *communion*—the *Whoopee!* of living for God. I ache when I see churches turn it into some somber, sad moment. To remember the gracious, forgiving Jesus sets fireworks off in my heart. If anyone ever chooses to remember me, I hope they do it with joy and laughter. I think Jesus wants the same.

Fourth, communion is not a *reward* for having reached a certain age or joined a certain church. It is simply one's memory having a party over Jesus. It is a declaration of whose side you are on. It is a smile that remains when all the rest of ourselves has disappeared (I borrow from *Alice in Wonderland*). Communion is for anyone who wants to say, "I believe and I belong." It is not limited to those in good standing in some institution of religion. Often people ask me at what age they should permit their children to participate in communion. The answer is simply, "At whatever age you want them to remember Jesus."

Fifth, some churches practice what is called *closed communion.* They permit no one except members of their group/denomination or local church to partake with them. By this act they recognize only themselves as Christians. This is dangerously close to partaking *unworthily* which Paul warned against in 1 Corinthians 11 by not discerning or recognizing the body of Christ. How sad it is when people pull their cloaks around them and shut themselves away from the awesome, growing body of Christ in the world. How dangerous, too, since we drink *judgment on ourselves* when we do.

Sixth, I have been in conferences where various church officials of high standing were present. They were free to participate in all parts of the meeting except communion. I realized that this moment was a watershed. If they partook in any communion except from their own hands, they were admitting that others beside themselves were saved and had direct access to God. In spite of all the talk of getting together or calling us *separated brethren*, until they take communion officially from us, they don't recognize us as Christians and they don't recognize what we do as communion.

Seventh, people have asked me if we should let nonbelievers participate in communion and I have heard preachers urge nonbelievers to refuse to participate. Why would a nonbeliever want to participate, anyway? Who are we to tell them to abstain, anyway? Maybe this is the nonbeliever's way of saying, "I now believe." I have come to the conclusion that by the grace of God, I will never say, "No." I want to keep the hand of invitation extended. If we have the keys to the kingdom, let us use them to open up the door. Freely we have received, let us freely give.

Eighth, people ask how often we should partake in communion. Churches have even split over whether it was to be weekly, monthly, quarterly. I don't know the answer to that. Jesus didn't say. He only said that as often as we do it, do it in remembrance of him. Maybe we should do it as often as we wish to remember him. Hmm.

Ninth, the *early church* in Corinth violated the use of communion seriously. So seriously that Paul warned them that they would be condemning themselves and that many of them had become sick, weak and had even died because of their misuse of communion. It was not because the wrong hands administered or because they let nonbelievers participate. Rather, it was because they were not recognizing who their brothers and sisters were. Paul told them to examine themselves; i.e., look into their hearts and see whom they were excluding from the kingdom or their brotherhood. Any time we don't recognize our brothers, we maim the body of Christ. Communion should be a time of repairing our relationships. One cannot *remember Jesus* without hearing him say, *"Love one another as I have loved you."*

Tenth, this is a new contract in which we are being paid as much as our best player. I marvel at the exorbitant contracts signed with sports figures. If I were on such a team, I would have to pay to play. However, what if they put such an exorbitant contract in front of me and said, "We are paying everyone on the team the same as our best player. Will you sign?" Who would hesitate to sign?

Finally, communion rings the bells of our expectancy. It reminds us that Jesus is returning and we will do this again with him at a great banquet. What a healing to our hearts!

Hopefully, we can now see that Jesus is God's open door with a smiling, welcoming face. The table behind him is ready. Welcome to the party! Let's eat!

Supreme Duty

Even as I write, major denominations are debating whether the church should seek to encourage people to, as they put it, "change faiths." If only, when denominations come to this point, they would have the courage and honesty to say, "We are no longer Christians. We shall now disband and distribute our assets to the poor." Actually, any denomination that exceeds 50 years in age has changed its emphasis to supporting its possessions rather than fulfilling its supreme duty. So what is that supreme duty? Hear Jesus:

He said to them, "Go into all the world and preach the good news to all creation." (Mark 16:15)
Then Jesus came to them and said, "All authority in heaven and on earth has been given to me. Therefore go and make disciples of all nations, baptizing them in the name of the Father and of the Son and of the Holy Spirit, and teaching them to obey everything I have commanded you. And surely I am with you always, to the very end of the age." (Matthew 28:18-20)

All men have a religion of some sort; consequently, all men can choose to be offended if we care to tell them the good news. Every time I read of evangelistic events being organized (and I have a few reservations about such *events*), I also read of whiners who tell the good news sharers to leave them alone. Many groups of people who have lost their interest in evangelism let such whiners discourage them.

I think what it reduces to is that we don't want to be persecuted, regardless of what Jesus said would happen to us. With some humor, I observe the studies of church growth organizations who want to be state-of-the-art in convincing people to join or attend church. Not one suggests that we be persecuted. Amazing, since the church grows most rapidly in times of persecution.

At any rate, while teaching a course on evangelism in a college, I asked each student to interview ten Christians and ask them how they came into the kingdom. Over 90% of those interviewed became Christians because an individual had shared the gospel with them. No one came because of a beautiful building. Only a few, very few, owed their new lives to media or large-scale evangelism events. When people love Jesus, they share him. When they are taught the Bible and become healthy sheep, they beget healthy sheep. Too simple!

Perhaps, then, the role of pastor/teacher in the church is to teach in such a way that people are so totally in love with God that they cannot be restrained from telling about him. When we lose our desire to bring people to Jesus, let us close our doors.

The Sabbath

An enduring debate swirls around which day we will call the Sabbath. The institutional church around the world basically ascribes that title to Sunday and that day, chosen because of the resurrection, becomes our day of meeting, worship and *rest*. As a child, I remember the constant question, "What can you do on Sunday?" If you saw *Chariots of Fire*, you will recall that the star, a strong Christian and world-class runner, refused to run Olympic races on Sunday.

Choosing Sunday as the day we gather to worship resulted in all manner of consequences, blue laws which permitted no one to do business on Sunday, legalisms that caused many to wonder if it was okay to even enjoy Sunday, theological splits for those who wanted to still observe Saturday.

So what is right? Actually, the Law found its fulfillment in Jesus, so he becomes the teacher who sets our understanding and gives us freedom. The first clue arrives with an apparent violation of Sabbath rules by Jesus and his apostles. When criticized for this brazenness, Jesus responds with words not realized before: *Then he said to them, "The Sabbath was made for man, not man for the Sabbath. So the Son of Man is Lord even of the Sabbath."* (Mark 2:27-28)

So now, Jesus begins to flesh out reasons for his actions among the people. He constantly healed people and seemed to gloat in doing so on the Sabbath. He flouted the rules of the Pharisees. Why would he do that? Simple. He was presenting the new Sabbath understanding. Then when he declares himself Lord of the Sabbath, understanding dawns. Jesus is our Sabbath and in him we find rest (Sabbath). No longer is one day different from the other when all of them are Sabbaths. Notice his clear call:

"All things have been committed to me by my Father. No one knows the Son except the Father, and no one knows the Father except the Son and those to whom the Son chooses to reveal him.

"Come to me, all you who are weary and burdened, and I will give you rest. Take my yoke upon you and learn from me, for I am gentle and humble in heart, and you will find rest for your souls. For my yoke is easy and my burden is light." (Matthew 11:27-30)

"For the Son of Man is Lord of the Sabbath." (Matthew 12:8)

He said to them, "If any of you has a sheep and it falls into a pit on the Sabbath, will you not take hold of it and lift it out? How much more valuable is a man than a sheep! Therefore it is lawful to do good on the Sabbath." (Matthew 12:11-12)

No longer does rest belong to a day, it now belongs to the creator. With his abiding presence in us, rest walks with us. Peace paves our way. Grace crowns us. Joy overflows us. Work is done for him. Rest comes from him. Every day is his and ours and no day need stand out from another except for one arbitrarily chosen (even Tuesday if we wish) to gather and worship.

Notice in the previous Scripture that *"All things have been committed to me...."* This means exactly what it says—all things. This includes rules about days and food and activities and, and, and. Since he defined rest (Sabbath) as only in him, then only in him (not a specific day) will we find Sabbath (rest). The logic is simple and clear. I also find that the more I know him and love him, the more this conflict weakens as an area of argument. *All things* is a wonderful and large area.

In its simple form, the Sabbath was for rest, simply rest. Since God rested after six days of awesome creativity, he mandated that man should also take that day of rest. Now, in this great day of the presence of our Lord, rest is not the product of a day, but the presence of the *Lord of the Sabbath* in our lives. Consequently, every day is Sabbath to the follower of Jesus, and it matters not what you call the day. He is our rest!

So, what if someone chooses to worship on Saturday or even on Sunday? Are they wrong? Not at all, unless they choose to make it something required for salvation or they choose to negate the meeting times of others who love God.

Sabbath was not a mold to form us but a decree to bless us. Now, we are blessed with all spiritual blessings in Jesus, including the peace and rest of eternal Sabbath. Now, because of the power of the Holy Spirit in our lives, we, by nature, remember our Lord and keep each of our days holy. Enjoy!

So, borrowing from the words of Jesus himself, "Go in peace...." If I may apply them now, *Meet in peace.*

Hearing His Voice

Everyone wants to hear from God, but those who say they have tend to make us wary and often weary. How can we know? Does God even want to talk to us now? Was the Church sent off on its merry way with only an ancient map? All of these questions are answered in the words of Jesus himself.

"I tell you the truth, the man who does not enter the sheep pen by the gate, but climbs in by some other way, is a thief and a robber. The man who enters by the gate is the shepherd of his sheep. The watchman opens the gate for him, and the sheep listen to his voice. He calls his own sheep by name and leads them out. When he has brought out all his own, he goes on ahead of them, and his sheep follow him because they know his voice. But they will never follow a stranger; in fact, they will run away from him because they do not recognize a stranger's voice."

Jesus used this figure of speech, but they did not understand what he was telling them. Therefore Jesus said again, "I tell you the truth, I am the gate for the sheep. All who ever came before me were thieves and robbers, but the sheep did not listen to them. I am the gate; whoever enters through me will be saved. He will come in and go out, and find pasture. The thief comes only to steal and kill and destroy; I have come that they may have life, and have it to the full.

"I am the good shepherd. The good shepherd lays down his life for the sheep. The hired hand is not the shepherd who owns the sheep. So when he sees the wolf coming, he abandons the sheep and runs away. Then the wolf attacks the flock and scatters it. The man runs away because he is a hired hand and cares nothing for the sheep.

"I am the good shepherd; I know my sheep and my sheep know me—just as the Father knows me and I know the Father—and I lay down my life for the sheep.

"I have other sheep that are not of this sheep pen. I must bring them also. They too will listen to my voice, and there shall be one flock and one shepherd." (John 10:1-16)

"...but you do not believe because you are not my sheep. My sheep listen to my voice; I know them, and they follow me." (John 10:26-27)

"I have revealed you to those whom you gave me out of the world. They were yours; you gave them to me and they have obeyed your word. Now they know that everything you have given me comes from you. For I gave them the words you gave me and they accepted them. They knew with certainty that I came from you, and they believed that you sent me." (John 17:6-8)

If we are under command to follow Jesus, then we certainly need a road map. Fortunately, we have two very reliable sources—his word (the Bible) and his voice. Jesus was very careful to only do what he saw the Father do and only say what he heard the Father say. He had trusted the Scripture delivered by the Holy Spirit through the ages and it follows that we can do no better.

Any religious group that decides the Bible is optional or untrustworthy should immediately change their name to some social or civic group and save the Church from fraud. No book so faithfully moves the heart and directs the soul. After years of study and ensuing degrees, I have found speculation rampant, searching intense, but Truth only in the Bible. God speaks to us through his Word. I rest in that.

Also, Jesus leaves no speculation about who is the center of his Church. If we get in, we come only through him—the door. If anyone chooses to identify with his Church, he must follow the Good Shepherd. If anyone says he has heard from God, the voice or direction must sound like Jesus.

Years ago, on a TV nature special about seals on an Alaskan island, I watched as they came ashore by the hundreds for birthing season. As I looked along that endless shore of brown humps, I thought, "When you have seen one seal you have seen them all." Then they gave birth to thousands more small brown humps. Then I thought, "When you have seen one seal pup you have seen them all."

When the mothers leave the island for a feeding time, the pups wander about and get mixed up. When the mothers return, they sort themselves out. How? Well, when seal pups are born, the mother and pup smell each other closely. When I saw that, I thought, "When you have smelled one seal, you have smelled them all."

Then the mother and pup bark at each other. When I saw that, I thought, "When you have heard one seal you have heard them all."

However, from that moment on, by smell and sound, they instantly know each other. I immediately think of Paul's statement that *We are to God the aroma of Christ....* (2 Corinthians 2:15) Then I remembered that scientists can tell us apart by the vibrations of our voice as surely as by our fingerprints. Perhaps there is something about the sound of the voice of Jesus that makes him instantly identifiable to us. There is!

When you look at the list of his servant nature which we have considered previously, it seems that this becomes a voiceprint for him. Any time we say we have heard from him, all results must match that voiceprint or consequently be an imposter. Likewise, any interpretation we make of the Scripture or any action we propose or any thought we have must be checked. If it does not match the nature of Jesus, the interpretation is wrong; the action is wrong; the thought must be abandoned. The written Word (the Bible) must never be interpreted in a way that violates the living Word (Jesus).

If I pray for him to dominate me as we are instructed to do in *The Lord's Prayer*, the more I will write his words and nature on my heart (my innermost being) so that I will stay on course. Without my saying it, others will think I have heard from God. Ah, success! We know this, too: He stays close enough to us to be heard: *"I am with you always."* (Matthew 28:20)

We listen, we hear, and we follow.

Simplicity

*"I have given you authority to trample on snakes
and scorpions and to overcome all the power of the
enemy; nothing will harm you. However, do not rejoice that the spirits submit to you, but rejoice that
your names are written in heaven."*

*At that time Jesus, full of joy through the Holy
Spirit, said, "I praise you, Father, Lord of heaven
and earth, because you have hidden these things
from the wise and learned, and revealed them to
little children. Yes, Father, for this was your good
pleasure.*

*"All things have been committed to me by my Fa-
ther. No one knows who the Son is except the Father, and no one knows who the Father is except
the Son and those to whom the Son chooses to reveal him."*

*Then he turned to his disciples and said pri-
vately, "Blessed are the eyes that see what you
see. For I tell you that many prophets and kings
wanted to see what you see but did not see it, and
to hear what you hear but did not hear it."* (Luke
10:18-24)

Few things damage the church more than the
complication and trivialization of theology. Often, when students ask me if I think they should
go to seminary, my response is that it is okay, but

they need to redeem the time they spend there. Of course, they are a bit shocked and ask me what I mean by that. The answer is simple. Seminaries never teach simple things. They tend to train seminarians to talk to other seminarians.

Consequently, to redeem the time, the student needs to attach himself to a local church and ask permission to teach a class of nine-year-old boys. If he can't teach what he has learned in seminary to them, then forget it himself. If he can, and it is meaningful to the boys, remember it.

If you will forgive my crudity, I also tell theology students that they spend four years taking in and taking in. They develop a theological constipation. Then they go to their first ministry post and have a *movement* that takes people years to clean up. When I would invite senior seminary students to speak for me in my lower-socioeconomic church, it tended to be disaster. Why? Because their training did not produce pastors who understood and taught the Scripture to hungry people. No, they are trained to be seminary professors. That is all that is exampled to them.

In the glorious glimpse into the very heart of our Lord in the Scripture above, his fullness of joy in the Holy Spirit grew from the simple fact that this incredible secret entrusted to us is child-size and, consequently, hidden from the intelligentsia.

This leads me to a statement that may seem harsh but is fully supported by observing the crowds that listened to Jesus: Any theology whose definition cannot be read and understood by a nine-year-old should be abandoned and declared heresy.

Simplicity gathers steam when we realize that much of the teaching of Jesus lifted children to a status formerly unrecognized. To offend a child proved deadly in the eyes of Jesus. He wanted them to have access to him. The angels constantly report to the Father about their treatment. Jesus greatly valued children:

"See that you do not look down on one of these little ones. For I tell you that their angels in heaven always see the face of my Father in heaven." (Matthew 18:10)

Simplicity certainly fits the nature of Jesus. Children represented the weakest in society. Power, in the Kingdom of God, flows from strength to weakness as we see in Jesus' use of power in the footwashing scene of John 13. Conversely, in the world, power gathers its strength from the weak. Thus, for Jesus to so value and protect children exhibits basic Kingdom logic.

From what I see in the teaching and action of Jesus along with the observations of my years, I believe that if you can't make it simple, it means that you do not know it. Those who complicate matters speak out of ignorance.

The Level Field

O ne of the statements I often heard preachers make as I, from the first Sunday I was alive, made church my home was, "The ground is level at the foot of the cross." The meaning was unmistakable although its application, at least from my observation, escaped me. Indeed, Jesus, as we would put it, gave everyone the time of day, the benefit of the doubt. Any who approached him, regardless of motives, gained his ear. Even if you approach him by night because you don't want to be seen with him, you are granted an audience. If you call for him because you have the power to call for people and they come, he won't. The ground is level.

However, as I read the Gospels, I discover the ground is level in ways we may not have realized, even if we attempt to change the landscaping.

One such area has to do with divorce. God's displeasure with divorce stands irrefutable. Perhaps the main reason being that it creates adulterers according to Jesus. Here is how he puts it:

"Anyone who divorces his wife and marries another woman commits adultery, and the man who marries a divorced woman commits adultery." (Luke 16:18)

Based on this statement and current statistics, at least half of all marriages create adulterers. Those groups that limit their leaders to those who have been married only once find themselves with precious few candidates. Indeed, this tragedy called divorce has become, to many groups, the unpardonable sin. How can this be a level field? Here is the unnoticed leveler:

"But I tell you that anyone who looks at a woman lustfully has already committed adultery with her in his heart." (Matthew 5:28)

By this standard, Jesus turns every man into an adulterer. He said this to a group of arrogant Pharisees who believed that simply by following their own laws about divorce (by decree only) they were protected from any fault, regardless of the cruelty rendered to the powerless woman involved. Consequently, whether divorced or not, all hearts contain the sprouted seeds of adultery, thus all are in need of his redemption.

Notice the encounter of Jesus, Simon the Pharisee and a woman of the streets in Luke 7. The occasion was a meal to which Jesus was invited and then abused—not greeted, washed or seated. However, a woman of the streets enters and in her own way does the things Simon ungraciously refused to do. Jesus confronts Simon's pride and arrogance with a question about love. "If someone is forgiven a small debt and another a large debt, who will love the most?"

Simon got that answer correct, the one forgiven most. Jesus then stated that this woman's sins were many but she was forgiven. What Simon failed to note was that his own sins vastly exceeded the woman's. He simply, in his pride, failed to think so, therefore he thought that his forgiveness was small. Obviously he was unloving. Perhaps later, in his reflection, he realized that he had been brought down to level ground with the woman.

In Luke 10, when the disciples, sent out two-by-two, returned rejoicing that the demons were subject to them in Jesus' name, Jesus issued his only *cooling* order. *"...do not rejoice that the spirits submit to you, but rejoice that your names are written in heaven."* The demons would still be subject to them, but the rejoicing should be over what God has done for them in salvation, not in what they were doing for God. Level ground.

In Jesus' day, women were regarded as little more than property. A Pharisee would move to the other side of the street rather than risk being contaminated by meeting a woman. How would you feel as a woman if, married to a Pharisee, you heard this prayer every morning: "I thank you, God, that you did not make me a slave, a dog, or a woman"? Women were not permitted to be educated. Tradition proclaimed that they could learn nothing. Women were not allowed to be witnesses in court. Men said they could not be believed. They were not permitted to participate in religious activity. The best they had was a place away from the meeting room and out of sight.

Now, Jesus arrives and establishes an entirely different value for women. He, their creator, sees them as persons of equal value. He expresses his opposition to the Pharisaical approach in dramatic ways.

First, he permits Mary to sit at his feet (Jesus Christ University) and learn, much to the chagrin of Martha. Keep in mind that universities of that day were not institutions, but outstanding teachers. Second, women were the first witnesses to the resurrection. Third, to a Samaritan woman of disrepute (three strikes!) he first announces that he is the Messiah. *Women's liberation,* however you wish to define it currently, has no clue as to how much it owes Jesus. Level ground.

In another chapter of this book, we see how deeply Jesus values children, making them the foundation of the Kingdom. Level ground.

Every mountain is made low in an extraordinary statement by Jesus about how we view and treat people: *"I tell you the truth, whatever you did for one of the least of these brothers of mine, you did for me."* (Matthew 25:40)

Level ground.

Candidates

The world divides people into very separate camps: royalty and peasants, rich and poor, powerful and powerless, strong and weak, smart and ignorant, beautiful and plain. God lumps them all into one category: loved and invited. The announcement of the birth of Jesus left no doubt about whom he considers candidates.

First of all, a band of shepherds heard the first announcement. One must realize that these shepherds were about the lowest on the social scale. No one trusted shepherds. They were like your friendly, local burglars. When they went through town, things tended to disappear. No worse group could have been chosen for the announcement unless God was making a statement—a statement that his Kingdom reached from the lowest all the way up.

Also, the angels announced that Jesus' birth would be good news to *all people*. Now, how many do you think are included in the word *all*? Immediately, we realize that God's love for people is thorough and complete. No one is automatically excluded from the reach of his arms. Indeed, God mocks the false divisions of mankind.

When the disciples sought to repel children and their mothers, perhaps in an attempt to protect Jesus from the crowd demanding his time, an irritated Jesus rebuked the disciples and announced a basic tenet of his Church, *"Let the little children come to me, and do not hinder them, for the kingdom of God belongs to such as these."* (Mark 10:14) How much plainer can it get? God obviously values people, people, people and abhors categories.

Notice, also, a great parable of the Kingdom when Jesus told the story of a king inviting people to a feast. It appears that the first invitations went out to people of means and importance. That is logical since they tend to be at the forefront of communications. However, they unanimously rejected the invitation for the most frivolous of reasons. Was Jesus trying to make a point here? But follow on. The banquet is not canceled. Indeed, he tells his servants to go into the highways and hedges and compel or convince people to come to his banquet. He wanted the tables full.

Highways and hedges? That doesn't sound much like the elite of the world (who happen to be very few). Indeed, it sounds like the opposite. Do you suppose Jesus was trying to make a point here? True, the elite and educated might hear the news first, but obviously, they will be the first to reject. It takes far less convincing to get someone from the hedges to attend the king's banquet. To these *hedges people*, the opportunity for such a gathering exceeds all logic. The elite would find their presence repugnant giving them further excuse for refusing the invitation.

When in the synagogue of Nazareth, his home town, Jesus announced that he fulfilled the prophecy of Isaiah concerning the *anointed one*. The condensation of that *anointed* passage, related to us by Luke, describes the beneficiaries of his anointing:

"The Spirit of the Lord is upon me, because he hath anointed me to preach the gospel to the poor; he hath sent me to heal the brokenhearted, to preach deliverance to the captives, and recovering of sight to the blind, to set at liberty them that are bruised, To preach the acceptable year of the Lord." (Luke 4:18-19 KJV)

How obvious the list! Poor, brokenhearted, captives, blind, bruised (oppressed), out-of-favor people. Not one *higher-up* makes the list. Don't you ever wonder why? We live in a world of massive pain in the massive majority who are massively covered by the description of what the anointing did to Jesus. God cares about people!

Only one group of people seemed to receive the wrath of Jesus—the religious leaders. They, rather than open the doors of God to people, shut them and abused the people. Mercy was a quaint and unstudied concept to them. Jesus spared nothing in expressing his disdain for them. He called them snakes in the grass, hypocrites, beautifully painted tombs. Maybe Jesus was trying to make a point about who might not be in his Church. Wait a minute! These are church leaders! Ouch! Perhaps we pay too little attention to the corruption that comes to those in religious power.

Driving Forces

Jesus' method of teaching rested primarily in interaction and response and parables. Several times, with the apostles, he established principles because of their questioning. Often he responded to their actions—actions that frequently exposed their humanity. On one occasion, he dealt with three forces that drive us, thus establishing part of the constitution of the Church. Those three forces are emotion, greed and family approval.

As they were walking along the road, a man said to him, "I will follow you wherever you go." Jesus replied, "Foxes have holes and birds of the air have nests, but the Son of Man has no place to lay his head."

He said to another man, "Follow me." But the man replied, "Lord, first let me go and bury my father." Jesus said to him, "Let the dead bury their own dead, but you go and proclaim the kingdom of God."

Still another said, "I will follow you, Lord; but first let me go back and say good-by to my family." Jesus replied, "No one who puts his hand to the plow and looks back is fit for service in the kingdom of God." (Luke 9:57-62)

The first character in the story to encounter Jesus expressed strong emotion about following him *wherever you go.* Sometimes the intensity of feeling or lack of it decides whether people will attend certain churches or participate in the Christian world in any way. Frequently, after a time of intense emotion related to church services, feelings can actually fall precipitously to depression.

Jesus, knowing that emotions are not the basis for following him, gave this man a strange yank on his chain: "I have no place to lay my head." In the glow of fellowship and singing, excitement can and perhaps should run high; however, some of the prices of following Jesus run just as high as the excitement.

When the conveniences and comforts of home are absent, does our loyalty weaken? If we cannot take along our special pillow or find a familiar fast-food place nearby, do we have second thoughts? If organs and padded pews and stained-glass windows are replaced by drums, benches and gathered brush, will we still sense the Spirit? Is our relationship one of nostalgia or a current one?

These are the hard questions that are better answered early than late in one's relationship. Indeed, in one of his parables Jesus described seed thrown on stony ground this way:

"Others, like seed sown on rocky places, hear the word and at once receive it with joy. But since they have no root, they last only a short time. When

trouble or persecution comes because of the word, they quickly fall away." (Mark 4:16-17)

Perhaps, at best, we should view our emotions as neutral or with great suspicion, carefully submitting them to verification by Scripture. At worst, feelings cause us to fall away.

So, emotions are not the foundation of the Kingdom, but simply fringe benefits with random occurrence. They are received with gratitude but not used as building materials.

To the second person, Jesus gave a harder response. This man wanted to follow Jesus but first wanted to bury his father. Now, that sounds like a good family value on the surface. Once past the surface, we see reality—this man's father was not yet dead.

Remember that in those days, they did not embalm people so they could be made to look *natural* and be shown for days. No, whenever someone died, they were buried the same day. So, if this man's father had died, he would not have been there with Jesus, he would have been already burying his father. What then is this man saying?

This man is saying that he wanted to go home and stay until his father died and he had secured his inheritance. With this statement, he joined the greedy systems of the world. Jesus confronted his greed and told him not to join their death-drive for security. Any religious system that builds on greed forsakes the foundation of Jesus and drinks the poison of death.

To the third person, the answer of Jesus hit the hardest. This man wanted to go and say *good-bye* to his family. Now, this sounds like the kind of person you would feature in Christian magazines. Here is a man who apparently understands proper family dynamics. Well, listen to what Jesus says to him, *"Whoever puts his hand to the plow and looks back is not fit to serve in the kingdom."* Whoa! Is Jesus that insensitive to family values?

Frankly, Jesus was insensitive to cultural family values. I know this is troubling, but we can see that it is true. This man requested the right to get family approval. In that culture, *good-byes* never flowed to a family member whose actions failed to meet family approval. Family approval was not then nor is it now a foundation stone for service in the Kingdom of God. Indeed, how many of your friends and family would even be in the Kingdom if dependent on family approval?

I have known young people freed from drugs by the power of God whose parents went ballistic. They informed their children that they understood them better when they were on drugs but they didn't understand this *Jesus stuff*. Fortunately, the young people preferred God over parental or family approval.

Perhaps this is why the church struggles harder to grow in those areas where tradition is strongest. Too many approvals to be gained. Too many "What will people think?" statements to overcome. In places where such tradition breaks down, people more readily accept the good news of

Jesus. Their traditions, they find, do not save them.

So, emotions must be hitched to biblical surety. Greed must be subverted to and replaced by giving. Family approval must be replaced by courageous decisions. Such is the Kingdom.

Mothers and Brothers

If you look to the words of Jesus for a theology of family, prepare for trouble. Jesus was harsh on family as we know it. If you wish, you may begin with his own genealogy. Here was the one who could choose his own blood line descending the ages through one righteous person after another. Instead, his ancestry is filled with baser sorts. Why would he do that? Perhaps he is saying something about our vain search of our heritage. Perhaps.

His forerunner was born, not to a young, up and coming, energetic priest and his wife, but instead to an old couple—a priest, who because of his having no children, could only be deemed a failure. Why would God have that to be so? Perhaps to confront our vanity.

Jesus himself is born, not to an established couple with a record of righteousness, but instead to a (perhaps) 15-year-old girl not yet married. Why would that be? Perhaps God wants to show us the true depths of his grace in whom he uses.

Notice in Mark 3 the following scene:

When Jesus returned to the house where he was staying, the crowds began to gather again, and soon he and his disciples couldn't even find time to eat. When his family heard what was happening, they tried to take him home with them. "He's out of his mind," they said. (Mark 3:20-21 NLT)

Do you realize the implications of his own family (mother included) thinking that their Messiah boy had lost his mind? Such arrogance on their part! Obviously, Mary did not understand the heart of Jesus. Power (being his mother) can corrupt in subtle ways.

So they go to bring him home. When they arrive at where Jesus is teaching, listen to this surprising (yet foundational) response:

A crowd was sitting around him, and they told him, "Your mother and brothers are outside looking for you." "Who are my mother and my brothers?" he asked. Then he looked at those seated in a circle around him and said, "Here are my mother and my brothers! Whoever does God's will is my brother and sister and mother." (Mark 3:32-35)

Put yourself in Mary's shoes and you hear this question from within the crowd, *Who is my mother?* A staggering question.

It is inescapable that this is a slap at his own family, including his mother. Indeed, Jesus apparently needed to confront her and some erroneous beliefs about her on more than one occasion to avoid undue veneration of Mary (!!). He also had to resist what appears to be increasing attempts at domination on her part. This event is difficult to believe and more difficult to reconcile. Jesus was establishing a new family—the family of God.

We are all born into natural but temporary families. I never asked to be an Erwin. I had no choice. When I was born, the doctor said, "That looks like an Erwin," then he slapped me! However, there will be Erwins I won't likely see after this fleshly life is over. At best, this Erwin family is temporary.

I am now part of a new family that is eternal. It is a family of choice—one into which I am born (again) and given a whole new spiritual genetic strain. Which family is superior and worthy of greater love? Obviously, the spiritual family.

Now, let us come to grips with a most difficult passage about family. Jesus said, *"If anyone comes to me and does not hate his father and mother, his wife and children, his brothers and sisters—yes, even his own life—he cannot be my disciple."* (Luke 14:26) Hard to believe that Jesus would make such a statement. Jesus is simply saying that you must love him more than your family.

To any follower of Jesus, to any recipient of his grace, this view causes no wonder or upset. Does this mean that we actually love our families less because we are Christians? Certainly not! As Christians we actually love our families more than before because of our excelling love of Jesus and gratitude to him for accepting us into this new family. However, we are no longer in bondage to our former family and can reject manipulation by them. Indeed, our relationship with God as our

Father brings health to temporary family situations that might have been filled with deadly relationships such as manipulativeness. You simply love God much more than you have ever or ever could love your family.

Jesus fought manipulation. When he didn't join the return party from Jerusalem, his parents frantically hunted him, finding him in the Temple of all places(!) reasoning with and highly impressing the teachers. His parents rebuked him (amazing that they would do that to the Messiah) and found themselves rebuked for not understanding that he was only doing what they had taught him to do.

Remember that at the wedding of Cana, Jesus' mother pushed herself on to his power and urged him to do a miracle. Why? Well, she was a pushy mom and a little intoxicated by the power of being *Mother of God*. Also, she, as well as her other sons, had no clue about timing, and, again, did not understand the heart of Jesus. Though he continued with the miracle, Jesus had to rebuke her. However, we must note at that time, we do hear the conciliatory and final recorded words of Mary, *"Do whatever he tells you."* (John 2:5)

Finally, proving that the rebuke never lessened the love for his family (though he loved his heavenly Father with all his heart, soul, mind and strength), Jesus gives his mother to John. Why John? Well, John had a pushy mother, also, and would know how to relate to her. Interestingly enough, had Mary been who some think she is, the New Testament would be filled with quotes from her. Instead, it is painfully silent. Surely that gives us insight that she was respected but not relied upon by church leaders. This is simply proof that God's grace (even in choosing a temporary family) extends to all, despite personal weakness.

When someone touts *family values* in our day, my mind automatically wonders, "Which family does he mean? Does he mean his temporary family?" I don't know the values of his temporary family, but I do know the values of the family of God.

So here are the implications: When we become followers of Jesus, we are born into an eternal and superior family. The greatest glory is when your temporary family also joins the family of God. Because of its permanence, we work hard to develop the relationships in our new, eternal family (we also call this fellowship). The relationships in our new eternal family improve and give health to our relationships with our temporary family. The relationships of the eternal family give strength to what we call the Church. Indeed, this new family *is* the Church.

Membership

Once we understand the spiritual genetics and new-family system of the Church, the thought of local membership borders on the humorous. Legal systems of government developed the whole concept of membership. If the church is going to be a state recognized entity, some form of membership must be developed. Also, if people wish to have tax deductions for their contributions, the church must be recognized by the state.

Suppose a fellowship decides to forego being recognized by the state. That is acceptable as long as you don't plan to own property. The moment you do, you must become some sort of corporation recognized by the state in order to sign legal papers. The rules require experts and even they do not understand all the legal ramifications of being a church. They certainly don't understand the spiritual concepts.

Membership really has nothing to do with our relationship with Jesus. Family does, though. The concept of joining and then *moving* our membership to some other structure has only legal significance, not spiritual. When you become a Christian—born into the Family of God—you are already a member. However, Jesus did issue a *membership card.* We look at it now.

The Card

Nothing poisons the Kingdom of God more than the requirements men place on each other. Every generation in every culture falls naturally into some form of law. Whatever the form of law developed, everyone falls short.

Many churches and religious groups require a signature on a card that promises they will do this or will not do that. Some require that they believe a set of statements and/or definitely do not believe certain theologies; however, *not one,* not one requires that we love each other. Why? Religious

requirements abandon love and become the natural end of a fallen church.

The simple fact is that the entry requirements
of heaven are vastly beyond any best effort of
mankind. Even the apostles seemed to recognize
this dilemma. When the man we call *The Rich
Young Ruler* asked Jesus what he needed to do to
inherit eternal life, Jesus answered by quoting
parts of the Ten Commandments. Though he had
maintained, or so he thought, such a holy lifestyle
since his youth, Jesus quickly discerned his selfishness and greed.

Informed that he should sell what he had, give
all to the poor and come follow Jesus, this rich
young man hit a wall he couldn't climb and went
away sad. Jesus then said to his apostles that it
was harder for a rich man to go to heaven than for
a camel to go through the eye of a needle. Peter
recognized the height of that wall and responded
that it was impossible to be saved. That was one of
his more brilliant statements.

Jesus was not talking about a small gate in the
Jerusalem wall that a camel could go through
only on his knees with nothing on his back. That,
though difficult, is not impossible, and, further-
more, there is not nor has there ever been such a
gate in the Jerusalem wall.

So, when Jesus said *"a camel through the eye of
a needle,"* he meant *a camel through the eye of a
needle.* Now, I don't know if you have ever tried to
push a camel through the eye of a needle! It can be
done, but you must grind him up very fine to get
him through. I don't think there is much market

for ground camel, and, as C. S. Lewis put it, "He feels all bloody and strung out when you finish." Frankly, it is harder for *any* man to go to heaven than for a camel to go through the eye of a needle.

Perhaps one can possess things and not be possessed by them, but I believe we must view them with the same attitude Paul did—dung! If we do, we won't get too attached nor will we brag that we have more *dung* than anyone else! Indeed, this encounter with the rich man as well as the observation that his audience consisted of *common people* indicates strongly that the Kingdom is supported by poor people and not by the rich.

When rich people contribute, they tend to desire recognition. Depending upon the funds of a rich person in the congregation is a countdown to division, perhaps destruction. The Kingdom is mostly made up of and supported by the poor.

We use numerous methods to assert that we are Christians. Everything from past (and infant) baptism to membership cards, T-shirts and bumper stickers. The confusion keeps us searching for ways to discern a person's relationship with the Lord. Often, I ask people with whom I am conversing to tell me their spiritual history or I ask where they fellowship. These questions produce telling results.

So, Peter's observation is true. This task is impossible. Jesus fine-tuned by saying, *"With man this is impossible, but with God all things are possible."* (Matthew 19:26)

What did Jesus signal for card carriers in his Kingdom? He tells us:

"A new commandment I give unto you, That ye love one another; as I have loved you, that ye also love one another. By this shall all men know that ye are my disciples, if ye have love one to another." (John 13:34-35 KJV)

The requirement of Jesus that we love one another reaches beyond our capabilities. When he set love of one another as the identifying membership card, he built a wall not one of us could climb, unless, of course, he somehow enabled us in our inadequacies. That enabling becomes the secret treasure trove of the Kingdom. Nothing Jesus requires falls short of his enabling spirit. Only when man alone (the unredeemed, carnal one) faces the requirement does it become impossible.

So, indeed, there are requirements, impossible ones, for being in the Kingdom, but there are provisions, unimaginable ones, that provide our ticket.

Jesus authorized *all men* to issue the test of my membership. I would rather simply show them my card! Perhaps you have heard (or said) this defensive statement: "You can't judge me. You only see the outside. God sees my heart." True. However, an experience of mine taught me a deep lesson.

When we first moved to the West Coast, the house we bought had a peach tree in the yard. I was glad, because I like peaches. We lived there for five years. That tree looked like a peach tree and smelled like a peach tree, but it never had a peach! I decided to cut it down. What if, as I approached it with a hatchet, it spoke to me and said, "Don't cut me down. In my heart I am a peach tree."

I would answer, "I didn't plant you for peach hearts, but for peach fruit." I cannot escape the observation of others.

More troublesome to me was Jesus' statement to love, *as I have loved you.* When I think of the love of God, I think of being crucified. Frankly, that has never been an attractive option to me. However, when Jesus made this statement, he had not yet been crucified and he is speaking past tense—love one another as I already have loved you. The immediate question—how had he loved them?

Interestingly enough, John 13, from which this command comes, begins this way:

It was just before the Passover Feast. Jesus knew that the time had come for him to leave this world and go to the Father. Having loved his own who were in the world, he now showed them the full extent of his love.

So, now he showed them just how much he loved them, the full extent of his love—he loved them to the end. How did he do it? Just moments later he rises from the table and does the most servant-hearted, others-centered action. He washes the apostles' feet. That simple act reveals the deep secret of love and the very nature of Jesus himself. The love that he exampled overflowed from a heart that turned toward others, that *agape* type of love that so uniquely attaches itself to Christianity and defines it.

Footwashing is not part of our greeting rituals of today nor does it embody the same meanings. Here, rather than establish a sacrament or develop a liturgy, Jesus simply exampled an attitude and a lifestyle—servanthood.

So, Jesus does not call me to great or gushy feelings (those have their place and time), but he calls me to a specific type of action fueled by the servant heart. Amazing, but simple. This system certainly simplifies record keeping on the roll books.

The Baptism

"Therefore go and make disciples of all nations, baptizing them in the name of the Father and of the Son and of the Holy Spirit." (Matthew 28:19)

The only thing Jesus taught about baptism was that we were to do it. Obviously, this very public act signals a change of ownership in our lives and provides identification. He also taught that we baptize *in the name* of the Father, Son and Holy Spirit. If you recall the chapter entitled "In The Name," you may remember that this name description fits Jesus, the Father and the Spirit; consequently, whatever you choose as a baptismal formula, we are baptizing into the same compassion, grace, patience, mercy and forgiveness that defines our Lord. What a great ID.

Neighbors

The religious leaders in their disdain of Samaritans taught that they were less than human therefore not actually neighbors. Nationalism shaped the actions of Israel more than God's commands. For that reason, the teaching of Jesus that we call *The Good Samaritan* spoke not only to the narrowness of the religious leaders but also to the nature of the Church.

But he wanted to justify himself, so he asked Jesus, "And who is my neighbor?" In reply Jesus said: "A man was going down from Jerusalem to Jericho, when he fell into the hands of robbers. They stripped him of his clothes, beat him and went away, leaving him half dead. A priest happened to be going down the same road, and when he saw the man, he passed by on the other side. So too, a Levite, when he came to the place and saw him, passed by on the other side.

"But a Samaritan, as he traveled, came where the man was; and when he saw him, he took pity on him. He went to him and bandaged his wounds, pouring on oil and wine. Then he put the man on his own donkey, took him to an inn and took care of him. The next day he took out two silver coins and gave them to the innkeeper. 'Look after him,' he said, 'and when I return, I will reimburse you for

any extra expense you may have.' Which of these three do you think was a neighbor to the man who fell into the hands of robbers?"

The expert in the law replied, "The one who had mercy on him." Jesus told him, "Go and do likewise." (Luke 10:29-37)

The questioner, an expert in the law, who prompted this story had an unusually good grasp of correct theology but not enough to grasp the Kingdom. Jesus confronts his narrowness with a story they all understood.

Nothing speaks of the condition of this world more than a person who went down to Jericho and fell among thieves who stripped and beat him, leaving him half dead. Everyone at some point or as a condition of life feels that he has fallen among thieves. Such is the way of this fallen world. The only question is, "Who will help?"

Quickly we see that the religious leader, the priest, passes by much too busy to get involved and much too cautious to touch a body that might be dead, causing him to be unclean, thus removing him from his duties. Close behind him came the Levite, the religious bureaucrat. Although he might be closer to the people than the priest, this is not in his job description. He scurries along toward the temple, glad that his work is cleaner than caring for half-dead people.

Ah, now the plot thickens. Surely the tension reaches massive proportions at the next words: *A Samaritan came along...and had compassion on him.* What a blow to Jewish national pride, that compassion would belong to a Samaritan! Not only that, he immediately began the caring and healing process, almost as if he traveled with emergency supplies for the robbed and beaten. Who else could Jesus have been talking about but himself? He placed himself as the despised yet compassionate one.

Not only did the Samaritan take immediate healing action, but transported the man to an inn where the process of recovery could be completed, paying liberally for the stay and promising all that was needed upon his return. What more can this inn and innkeeper be than the Church? Only Jesus can save and heal, but he leaves the recovery and discipling process up to us promising full reward upon his return. Just as that innkeeper trusted that the Samaritan would keep his word, so we trust that Jesus shall return and keep his word.

So, we are the innkeepers who harbor, protect and meet the recovery needs of all those brought to us by Jesus. What a horrible tragedy if we merely continue the thieving and beating.

Organization

Differing methods of organization constitute the primary separation of most denominations.

Some groups design church government after the United States government. They have a president, the pastor; a congress, the board; and the supreme court, the annual business meeting. These churches are congregationally centered and vote on everything, even the pastor. The weakness of this system is precisely the problem of the United States government. You have three branches of government designed to be checks and balances. They are loyal adversaries. Also, when such voting occurs, just as in the United States system, political parties form and power centers learn to control. Voting, by the way, is also called "division of the house."

Some churches are governed by a supreme leader who, though he delegates some local decisions, is in total control and decides who serves where. These powerful individuals tend to lean toward either conservatism or liberalism and their choices of local leaders determine the lean (or death) of the denomination.

Another style of government is by group leadership. The groups (elders, perhaps) are chosen either by vote or appointed, sometimes for life. If the eldership has a prescribed number, true spiritual leadership in the church may be inadequate to fill the positions (if indeed spiritual leaders are truly electable) to the point that carnal leaders form the majority.

What system did Jesus choose? If you watched the apostles, you concluded that life in the church is a constant power struggle. In the Gospels, their most common activity was arguing over who was the greatest. In Matthew 20:20-28, James and John, apparently convinced that Jesus was the Messiah, were equally convinced that he was a poor administrator and didn't know how to organize this outstanding new movement. Their solution? Hire *Momma* to be a lobbyist. She sought the top two positions in his Kingdom for her sons. Jesus informed them that they *would* suffer and die for him but the positions were not his to give. This effort of James and John resulted in another fight among the apostles.

This encounter informs us that Jesus must not be too interested in organization. What, then, was his emphasis? Identifying and empowering leaders! Perhaps the organic body nature of his Church meant that he did not want anything other than the local and the relational.

For the most part, church organizations and constitutions are designed to keep the group going and the property maintained regardless of whether the group continues to follow Jesus. I often humorously comment that most groups have enough safeguards and spare money to keep them going long after the rapture of the Church.

So, it seems that organization is a problem we develop and not one Jesus cared to participate in. Perhaps the inadvertent methods of the early church can help us. Since church buildings and larger gatherings did not occur until 300 to 400 years after Christ, the church in its early and highly successful growth revolved around homes. Why might that be so powerful?

First, homes can only get a limited number of people together so that means that everyone gets to know everyone. Notice that Jesus chose the twelve to be *with him*. Since everyone knows everyone, a certain degree of accountability and trust grows. Further, in such home gatherings, everyone gets to pray and everyone gets to be prayed for. Also, everyone gets to serve and everyone gets to be served.

At such places, the size permits discussion and application of the Bible. Thus, no one leaves without their needs being met. No special equipment is needed, so it is inherently inexpensive. That means the funds gathered can go to help others rather than pay mortgages. Sounds powerful.

However, the home system works only sparingly in the United States. Why? Well, we are not neighborhood oriented. Also, we are not under persecution. We have no shortage of gasoline, thus we travel miles to large gatherings that suit our fancy. So, all the things that might happen that we fear economically, might help the church mightily.

The requirement of Jesus to *lose our lives for his sake* applies to the church in all of its forms of organization as much as it does to the individual. However, the further the church removes itself from the individual by multiple strata of organization, the less the church can obey his command.

Showtime

"Be careful not to do your 'acts of righteousness' before men, to be seen by them. If you do, you will have no reward from your Father in heaven. So when you give to the needy, do not announce it with trumpets, as the hypocrites do in the synagogues and on the streets, to be honored by men. I tell you the truth, they have received their reward in full. But when you give to the needy, do not let your left hand know what your right hand is doing, so that your giving may be in secret. Then your Father, who sees what is done in secret, will reward you.

"And when you pray, do not be like the hypocrites, for they love to pray standing in the synagogues and on the street corners to be seen by men. I tell you the truth, they have received their reward in full. But when you pray, go into your room, close the door and pray to your Father, who is unseen. Then your Father, who sees what is done in secret, will reward you. And when you pray, do not keep on babbling like pagans, for they think they will be heard because of their many words. Do not be like them, for your Father knows what you need before you ask him." (Matthew 6:1-8)

We live in an advertising age. If it isn't showy, then it doesn't sell. Unfortunately, we have adopted this method for the church. We didn't get the method from Jesus, though.

Often, I have heard from those who wish to motivate us that the church is about 10 or 15 years behind the rest of the world. Their chiding includes: First, we are slow but catching up. Second, they will be glad to provide us with hyper-updates and drag us into the 21st century. Sadly, each new hype must be followed by an ever greater hype. I often wish we were 20 years behind and regressing.

When Jesus described his Kingdom, he used comparisons that we must not miss—leaven, a mustard seed. Notice that both are organic and both work quietly, but effectively, behind the scene. This logic fits with the prophecy about Jesus quoted in Matthew 12:

"He will not quarrel or cry out; no one will hear his voice in the streets. A bruised reed he will not break, and a smoldering wick he will not snuff out, till he leads justice to victory."

Some showcasers today try to turn Jesus into a radical rabble-rouser to support their own cause, however good or bad. These verses remove Jesus from such public agitation. Jesus, however, came quietly offering life. When the crowds sought to keep him in their own town in Luke 4:42, Jesus surprised them by revealing a must in his life—a must that would send him to what we would call "hick towns."

"I must preach the good news of the kingdom of God to the other towns also, because that is why I was sent."

Showtime for *The Church* is merely to make Jesus visible. Anything else is vanity.

Tares, Birds, Wolves

Perhaps the most difficult subject facing us, if we may borrow from a famous phrase, is that "Christianity makes strange bedfellows." Some events and public representatives, where we should be filled with joy, instead fill us with shame. Before we discuss this anomaly, let us take note of incredible Scripture:

Jesus told them another parable: "The kingdom of heaven is like a man who sowed good seed in his field. But while everyone was sleeping, his enemy came and sowed weeds among the wheat, and went away. When the wheat sprouted and formed heads, then the weeds also appeared.

"The owner's servants came to him and said, 'Sir, didn't you sow good seed in your field? Where then did the weeds come from?'

"'An enemy did this,' he replied. The servants asked him, 'Do you want us to go and pull them up?' 'No,' he answered, 'because while you are pulling the weeds, you may root up the wheat with them. Let both grow together until the harvest. At that time I will tell the harvesters: First collect the weeds and tie them in bundles to be burned; then gather the wheat and bring it into my barn.'"

He told them another parable: "The kingdom of heaven is like a mustard seed, which a man took and planted in his field. Though it is the smallest of all your seeds, yet when it grows, it is the largest of garden plants and becomes a tree, so that the birds of the air come and perch in its branches."
(Matthew 13:24-32)

In the first case, among the good and growing seed, an enemy also comes in and sows weed seeds. To the trained and discerning eye, their presence is obvious. Wheat and trees surely speak of fruitfulness and growth of the Kingdom. Tares (weeds) and birds are unmistakable problems. Tares are obvious deviations from the true wheat and true fruitfulness. Birds, which the trees, in this case, harbor, are (with the exception of the dove) almost always negative symbols in Scripture. What is Jesus trying to say? Simply this: The Kingdom will prosper but it will harbor in its fruitfulness people and actions that are not Kingdom. Indeed, they may be anti-kingdom.

Anyone who reads church history staggers away, reeling with embarrassment. How can the church be that way? Why doesn't God's judgment fall on those who, in the name of God, act evilly?

Apparently God is more interested in saving and caring for the Tree and the Wheat to give his attention to the birds and the tares. In almost all cases where I see individuals focus their attention on shooting the birds and pulling the tares, wheat is lost in the process. However, the tree will stand because it is built by Jesus. The tares will be obvious at harvest time because they stand as if to show off their greenness and their height long after the wheat has bowed its head in the brownness of its cycle and the fullness of its grain. If what was seen was the most important, one would only plant weeds; however, in the Kingdom as well as the wheat field, fruit (not looks) proves most profitable.

A living illustration was brought home to me some years ago. A major revival that occurred in the 1800's was subverted by bird shooters and tare pullers. Now, the denomination, known for guns of argument and exclusivity, continues to decline. I saw an honest history written of the revival by one of their own and the title of Chapter 2 was "What Went Wrong." How sad.

After a summer of working on the farm of my birth, spending grueling hours separating good wheat seed from weeds, I realized that the secret of good farming and fruit producing is to plant good seed. With my grandfather, I assisted in pulling the tares, because the loss of a wheat plant paled in the economic loss of harvesting so many corrupting weed seeds. Since in Jesus' day, all work was by hand and not machinery, he instructs the workers to leave the tares until harvest time when the true wheat cannot be damaged because the fruit has already been produced. The difference, as far as the Kingdom is concerned, amazes me. Jesus here teaches us that each individual is so valued by God that no discipline or judgment will come against others in a way that will damage the true believer's growth. Amazing!

This whole process of harvest and discipline yields interesting concepts for this thing we call the Church and especially for the institutionalized forms we call denominations. The primary concept is that any field that supports growth of good seed is going to have a few bad eggs (forgive the mixed metaphor) in it, but the eggs won't hatch.

In the second parable, Jesus informs us that the Kingdom grows even if only one seed, the smallest, is planted. Such is the power of the Word of God. In this story, a single tree rather than a field becomes the focus, a tree that grows from the tiniest seed to the greatest tree. Throughout history, such single moments, tiny missions, weakest individuals fuel impressive revivals that defy attempts to quantify them.

Jesus continues with another disturbing statement similar to the tares, *"the birds of the air come and perch in its branches."* What can be done about the birds? Jesus doesn't even hint at a defense. Again, amazing! What are the implications? Here are two. First, count on the fact that there is no such thing as a pure revival. The revival may be great, but it can never be pure as long as human beings and Satan hang around. Second, there is precious little deterrent to the birds.

Revivals past all fall into a state of what I call *prisoners of history*. As they grow and begin to detect tares and birds, they begin to organize in ways that evoke discipline and protection. Through this manner, they attempt to *preserve* the results of the revival. Here we observe the most amazing irony that no one seems to discern—the very act of preservation (institution-alization) violates the very nature of Jesus by try-ing to save our lives but instead insures death.

Why would this be a result of church growth? Perhaps the birds are a prophecy of Jesus about what every revival faces throughout history. In the course of any revival or church movement, such growth inherently attracts those who wish to identify with the exciting regardless of their per-sonal status with God. By the third generation, the great *tree* of the Kingdom harbors many who taint the beliefs and practices.

Jesus makes it clear that finding our lives means losing them rather than preserving them for his sake. Far greater damage is done in the preservation than from the birds or tares. Almost no one actually believes that statement. Attempt-ing to preserve the growth of the Kingdom, by its very nature, moves us into the activities that men esteem and that nauseate God.

Whenever my grandmother made *preserves*, I noticed that she only preserved fruit that was now dead. Perhaps that is comparison enough. But lis-ten to this insight: Trees (revivals) can grow and survive for quite some time, but institutions, in-cluding denominations, historically are corrupt and dead in 25 to 30 years and should be cut down. They are never treated with such disdain for only one reason—by now they are so esteemed of men or so financially profitable or so well landed that no one dares pick up an axe. Perhaps the harvest is over by the time the institution forms.

To our embarrassment, the richest organization in the world is *the church*. What does this wealth consist of? Buildings and land. What do they do with those buildings and land? Mostly boast. Dr. Charles Allen, a great Methodist pastor and man of God, when accepting the pastorate of a large church heard one of his men say, "Pastor, I simply view the church as a civic organization like the Rotary Club."

Allen responded, "No, you don't. I wish you would just give the church half the time you devote to your civic organizations. It would be revolutionary."

For this reason, God continues to raise up groups from wonderful and surprising revivals that grasp the original intent of Jesus and run with it—groups whose buildings will never be on the cover of any church magazine, groups who only want to worship him and share the good news.

Jesus introduced another vulnerability to the Church in this warning: *"Watch out for false prophets. They come to you in sheep's clothing, but inwardly they are ferocious wolves."* (Matthew 7:15) *In sheep's clothing* means that they may look and act and smell like sheep, at least enough to fool us and to wreak heavy damage on the flock. The foolproof way of discerning a wolf from a sheep is in what they eat. Sheep eat grass; wolves eat sheep.

Often one can differentiate on a larger scale whether wolves or sheep are in action. When new organizations or movements arise that seek their growth from other already-existing sheepfolds rather than bombarding the gates of Hell, I see the teeth of wolves.

Perhaps it should trouble us that 80% of what we call church growth statistically is simply the shifting of sheep from one fold to another. We *fishers of men* seem to be looking for someone's aquarium. Being a church boy, God privileged me to observe just about everything that has happened within and without religious walls. Certain titillating movements happen that appear, on the surface, to be new growth. Yet it looks to me like a set number of thrill-seeking people, like a giant amoeba, move from one amusement park to another.

In just the ten years prior to the writing of this book, there have been media-covered groups that first made us laugh uncontrollably, then made us shape our lives according to certified prophets and now they want us to fall unconscious for some unknown reason. Already the first two movements are dead and the last will die soon. The media doesn't cover the death, for which we can be thankful. None of these movements saved many from the gates of Hell. All of them drew from the rolls of the church.

Obviously, the Church suffers much from tares and birds and wolves; however, in God's economy, the wheat and the trees and the flock win and bear their fruit.

Yeast and Bewares

Jesus established the constitution of his Church in many ways and on different occasions. He knew the disciples couldn't grasp it all at once—they were slow learners. On one occasion he issued warnings that roll down to our day:

"Be careful," Jesus said to them. "Be on your guard against the yeast of the Pharisees and Sadducees. ...How is it you don't understand that I was not talking to you about bread? But be on your guard against the yeast of the Pharisees and Sadducees." Then they understood that he was not telling them to guard against the yeast used in bread, but against the teaching of the Pharisees and Sadducees. (Matthew 16:6, 11-12)

"Be careful," Jesus warned them. "Watch out for the yeast of the Pharisees and that of Herod." (Mark 8:15)

... Jesus began to speak first to his disciples, saying: "Be on your guard against the yeast of the Pharisees, which is hypocrisy." (Luke 12:1)

Three types of theology resided outside the boundaries of Jesus' Church—the Pharisees, the Sadducees and Herod. What did Jesus mean by this warning? It is easy to discern.

The Pharisees were the conservatives of their day, the traditional values people, the legalists. Founded in the 400-year period between the Old and New Testaments, their popularity created such a growth in numbers that they evolved into a political party which took over their congress—the Sanhedrin. Uh, deja vu? Over time, power corrupted them to the point that they worked harder to preserve their power than to preserve the Scripture. However, they had added considerably to the Scripture and most of the actions of their day arose from their long list of manmade rules. Further, they did a lot of public praying as they stole widow's houses.

Major problems (besides sheer corruption) accompany such legalism. First, it is impossible to write a law that you can keep. Every law brings about new lawbreakers. Now, if your spirituality (and others' view of it) depends on how you keep the rules (and you can't keep them), *keeping up appearances* becomes the order of the day. Of course, this is rank hypocrisy.

The twin brother of legalistic hypocrisy is mercilessness. The Pharisees cared little about people, only about their rules.

Jesus confronted another belief that traveled the same road as their lack of mercy. In Luke 5, Pharisees from every town in the region gathered in a house to observe Jesus—most probably to see what kind of threat he posed to their power. Although the power of God was present to heal, apparently none of the Pharisees availed themselves of this power, because they believed that if you were sick, it was because you sinned. Further,the Pharisees believed that God healed but only if you were sinless. Can you see their dilemma? If anyone asked Jesus to heal them, others would wonder, "What sin did he commit?"

Into this charged and crowded scene, a paralytic barges (compliments of some caring friends) through the roof. Jesus knew what the Pharisees believed, so he said to the man, "Your sins are forgiven."

At that moment, Jesus made him sinless. Do you see where this is going? So what did the Pharisees do? Their thoughts and murmurs were on this line, "Who does he think he is? Only God can forgive sin."

Yes! Now, to prove that he was God and to confront their lack of mercy, Jesus said to the man, "Arise. Take up your bed and walk." He did! Unfortunately, this incredible incident had little effect on the Pharisees. Hypocrisy and mercilessness are mean cohorts.

So, in this warning, Jesus prohibited his Church from being legalists and hypocrites.

The Sadducees were the liberals of their day. They didn't believe in resurrection or angels or much of anything that truly demonstrated God's power. They, too, represented a political party (second largest) in the Sanhedrin. Hmm. Deja vu all over again. They had the best relationship with the ruling Romans and, despite their smaller number, wielded the greater power with Rome. Rome forced the Sanhedrin to choose a Sadducee as the chief priest. Especially galled, the

Pharisees, being the majority in the Sanhedrin, would choose a Sadducee for Rome's sake then choose a Pharisee chief priest whom they would actually recognize.

Since the Sadducee moral structure lay on a much lower plane (typical of liberalism), and their view of Scripture lacked much loyalty (also typical of liberalism), Jesus warned his Church to avoid their theology and action. So now, we see that Jesus forbad either legalism or liberalism. Interesting.

One more group felt his warning—Herodians. Many believed that the proper use of politics would achieve their goals. If they could, by cooperating and gaining political power and influence, bring about more freedom and independence for the Jewish people—well, what could be wrong with that?

Jesus knew that the rules of politics never reached a moral plane. The rules of politicians are, "Get in power, stay in power and increase your power." They gladly use godly people to achieve their ends and drop them instantly when they prove useless for their own ends. This is a lesson the church has not learned to this day. How easily we violate the constitution of the Church and justify it every inch of the way. Does this mean that a Christian can never be involved in politics? No, it simply means that the Church cannot and no Christian politician should ever think that the hope of the Church lies in the power of politics.

Add to these groups the Zealots, the radical activists, and you complete the list that might be called the ruling elite. The Zealots were willing to do anything necessary to throw off the shackles of Rome, even if it cost thousands of Jewish lives as their efforts often did. Although Jesus left them out of the list of warnings, his statement that his Kingdom was *"...not of this world. If it were, my servants would fight..."* (John 18:36) certainly counts as excluding zealot goals.

Seeing the overview of these groups provides remarkable insight. All of these ruling groups were people of power and money. They also totaled only about 7% of the population. The remaining 93% were the *common people* or *the poor people of the land,* generally called the "Am Ha'aretz." The Pharisees and Sadducees viewed the poor people as cursed or unloved by God, thus their poverty. The Herodians and Zealots viewed them as mindless pawns. Since Jesus cares about people, little wonder that the *"...common people heard him gladly."* (Mark 12:37KJV)

So, Jesus warned that his Church would not be the location of legalism, liberalism or politics. Do you feel any pain as you think about this? Into what category do we fall? Let us emphasize again and again, "We are followers of Jesus."

Jesus Deserves the Best, Buildings and All

Often, as people describe some projected expensive program or building, I hear the term, "Jesus deserves the best," spoken as all the justification needed. What they really mean is, "I want my name placed on the very best." Just as often, names are placed on cornerstones of completed buildings that state, *For the Glory of God,* and then have a long list of important names.

Interestingly enough, almost all great buildings (especially including great cathedrals) are named after some individual, perhaps thought to be especially spiritual or saintly, rather than merely *God's Place.* Such names sound perilously like the builders of the Tower of Babel who wanted to *make a name for themselves.* Further, we tend to want these buildings to be located in prime real estate. Heaven forbid that they should not be noticed! This very question came up in a discussion of the most famous of all buildings:

Jesus left the temple and was walking away when his disciples came up to him to call his attention to its buildings. "Do you see all these things?" he asked. "I tell you the truth, not one stone here will be left on another; every one will be thrown down." (Matthew 24:1-2)

Rather humorous, it seems, that the disciples think Jesus had not noticed the stones. He did make them! However, the disciples were duly impressed, so much so that they wanted Jesus to join them in marveling. To their surprise, he took no pride in the awesomeness of the stones in the building of the temple. Instead, he declared that they would all be thrown down. Surely God would care more about *His house* than that! No, only the disciples (and the other religious types) found it impressive.

Perhaps, if Jesus disdains impressiveness, we should, too. Perhaps, if we must provide places for the faithful to congregate, they should be noticed for their utilitarian and economical nature rather than ornateness. Maybe there is something to be said for the warehouse, the storefront, the refurbished factory or the home. Perhaps we should view our buildings with the same fickleness that nature does or any of the shaking powers of the earth.

When God spoke from Mount Sinai his voice shook the earth, but now he makes another promise: "Once again I will shake not only the earth but the heavens also." This means that the things on earth will be shaken, so that only eternal things will be left. Since we are receiving a Kingdom that

*cannot be destroyed, let us be thankful and please
God by worshiping him with holy fear and awe. For
our God is a consuming fire.* (Hebrews 12:26-29
NLT)

Ultimately, the decoration of our hearts, the
bodies that contain us and that have become the
declared temple of the Holy Spirit become the far
more important building block to be noticed. The
sheer grace that has rescued us and the mercy
that has formed us make each of us a trophy of
God, a book yet to be written and read. If any con-
cern screams at us from the history of the Early
Church, it is that they were most concerned for
the welfare of the saints and not the welfare of any
buildings they owned.

From the very beginning, Jesus directed a
rather Spartan approach to kingdom building.
Notice his instructions:

*"As you go, preach this message: 'The kingdom
of heaven is near.' Heal the sick, raise the dead,
cleanse those who have leprosy, drive out demons.
Freely you have received, freely give. Do not take
along any gold or silver or copper in your belts; take
no bag for the journey, or extra tunic, or sandals or
a staff; for the worker is worth his keep."* (Matthew
10:6-10)

How easily Jesus could have stunningly
equipped them. If he could direct a fish to hold a
tax payment in his mouth to give to Peter, surely
he could supply all his preachers with expensive

tailored suits and every gathering with a cathedral sized building. We have put a period after *freely you have received* then added, *freely store*. However, just the opposite commands occurred. He instructs us to travel light.

Buildings, which mean so much to us in this day, can have a dramatic downside. Whenever the Gospel is preached where persecution is the order of the day, to build a Christian monument is a slap in the face of the culture and a target for any religious zealot or terrorist.

By contrast, house to house and neighborhood to neighborhood church growth becomes easy and economical. How much the fodder of the media when one of our church buildings burns down. We consider it such a loss. However, the true Kingdom hardly notices.

The Eternal Standard

And beginning with Moses and all the Prophets, he explained to them what was said in all the Scriptures concerning himself.

They asked each other, "Were not our hearts burning within us while he talked with us on the road and opened the Scriptures to us?" (Luke 24:27, 32)

What a missed opportunity that this incredible sermon remains unrecorded! What gold to hear Jesus himself interpret and teach the Scripture about himself. How disappointing that no record exists of this session. However, this Emmaus event exhibits the importance of the Bible, the Word of God, being confirmed and expounded by Jesus.

Indeed, throughout his anticipation, birth and life, Scripture held the highest place of trust and information. Even as Jesus wrestled with Satan in what we call "The Great Temptation," his reliance on the Scripture provided the final victory:

Jesus answered, "It is written: 'Man does not live on bread alone, but on every word that comes from the mouth of God.'" (Matthew 4:4)

Jesus assumed that whoever followed him would know and obey the Scripture. His words never replaced what had already been written, but only added final fulfilling portions. So sure was his understanding and dependence on the Word that he included *every word* (no editing or higher criticism here) and spoke as directly as possible: *"the Scripture cannot be broken"* (John 10:35) leaving no question about his view.

The quest of Jesus seemed to be focused on teaching the Word of God. Beside the Galilee, multitudes gathered to hear the word of God. (Luke 5:1) It may well be that when Jesus walked the earth, he was the only one actually teaching the Word of God. The Pharisees, as a back to the Bible movement between the testaments, so corrupted their message with mounds of additions and arbitrary interpretations that Jesus had to complain, *"you nullify the word of God by your tradition that you have handed down."* (Mark 7:13)

One of my favorite T-shirts has a picture of a Bible on it and simply states, "If you teach it, they will come." That certainly seemed to be true of Jesus. Further, he taught as *one having authority and not as the scribes.* (Matthew 7:29) This simply informs us that he never needed to quote any prior authority as he, being the authority, taught the Word in order to prove his logic and conclusions. This certainly caught the attention of the crowd, especially in Nazareth when he declared the Isaiah 61 passage as being fulfilled that day in their sight.

Additionally, Jesus never missed an opportunity to have the Word taught—with crowds, with parables, with the disciples—whatever method met the need. The disciples, sent to preach the Word, enjoyed the benefits of the miraculous only to prove the Word.

So many gathered that there was no room left, not even outside the door, and he preached the word to them. (Mark 2:2)

With many similar parables Jesus spoke the word to them, as much as they could understand. (Mark 4:33)

Then the disciples went out and preached everywhere, and the Lord worked with them and confirmed his word by the signs that accompanied it. (Mark 16:20)

The scattering of seed, so symbolic to the farming society, in a parable Jesus gave (confounding to the disciples—amazing!) was a parable of the Word and how it would be received or rejected or lost. The final glorious accomplishment:

"But the seed on good soil stands for those with a noble and good heart, who hear the word, retain it, and by persevering produce a crop." (Luke 8:15)

To our benefit, Jesus describes that good seed as the Word. Because the Word is good seed, even though it might be as tiny as a mustard seed, you can count on growth.

Jesus, again using the Word, limited even the adoration of his mother when a crowd member wanted to worship the one who nursed him:

He replied, "Blessed rather are those who hear the word of God and obey it." (Luke 11:28)

In like manner, he destroyed any further genealogical searchings and prevented any *holy family* thinking by building his own family around the Word:

He replied, "My mother and brothers are those who hear God's word and put it into practice." (Luke 8:21)

Salvation clearly revolves around the Word; and Peter, in that moment of discipleship uneasiness and departure, recognizes that eternity circles the words of Jesus:

"I tell you the truth, whoever hears my word and believes him who sent me has eternal life and will not be condemned; he has crossed over from death to life." (John 5:24)

Simon Peter answered him, "Lord, to whom shall we go? You have the words of eternal life." (John 6:68)

In this day, many people in academic scenes attempt to diminish and dissolve the Word. If the church is to be The Church, we must cling to the Bible and fervently hide it in our hearts. Otherwise, we are reduced to a mere pretense and should honestly declare our situation. Jesus foresaw this condition and clearly tells us the result:

"If anyone is ashamed of me and my words in this adulterous and sinful generation, the Son of Man will be ashamed of him when he comes in his Father's glory with the holy angels." (Mark 8:38)

But let us assume the best for those who share this book and follow the Founder of the Church in making the Word central to our belief and our message. That *best* hears the ultimate simplicity in Jesus' great *high-priestly prayer* of John 17:17, *"Sanctify them by the truth; your word is truth."*

The power of hearing and believing the message is contained in two marvelous statements of Jesus that make believing our most valuable choice:

"If you remain in me and my words remain in you, ask whatever you wish, and it will be given you." (John 15:7)

"You are already clean because of the word I have spoken to you." (John 15:3)

What great benefits simply by hearing and believing the Word. Then, as if to surround the power and benefits with a great heavenly set of parentheses:

In the beginning was the Word, and the Word was with God, and the Word was God. (John 1:1)

"Heaven and earth will pass away, but my words will never pass away." (Luke 21:33)

Little wonder that The Church should have the Bible in every teacher's hand and in every believer's heart. We are the people of The Book. Accordingly, we end this chapter with a most encouraging prayer from Jesus himself; one I believe the Father heard and continues to answer:

"My prayer is not for them alone. I pray also for those who will believe in me through their message, that all of them may be one, Father, just as you are in me and I am in you. May they also be in us so that the world may believe that you have sent me." (John 17:20-21)

Don't Worry, Be...

The silence of 400 years after the Old Testament breaks with two simple and repeatable words, *fear not*. Worry/anxiety is a function of fear, and fear is a form of bondage that Jesus seems to want broken. Throughout the Gospels, *fear not* interrupts normal human response. Normal response? Yes, worry and anxiety grip the hearts of uncountable masses—even in the church.

We live in a day that fosters so much agitation that you can understand the prediction of Jesus that men's hearts would fail them for fear (Luke 21:26). Little wonder that the best selling prescription drug on the market is to reduce anxiety. Fear focuses our thoughts on what will become of us and our situation, thus taking the controls back from God.

Anxiety is such a debilitating form of bondage that Jesus confronts it directly when he says:

"Look at the birds of the air; they do not sow or reap or store away in barns, and yet your heavenly Father feeds them. Are you not much more valuable than they? Who of you by worrying can add a single hour to his life?"

"And why do you worry about clothes? See how the lilies of the field grow. They do not labor or spin.

Yet I tell you that not even Solomon in all his splendor was dressed like one of these. If that is how God clothes the grass of the field, which is here today and tomorrow is thrown into the fire, will he not much more clothe you, O you of little faith?

"So do not worry, saying, 'What shall we eat?' or 'What shall we drink' or 'What shall we wear?' For the pagans run after all these things, and your heavenly Father knows that you need them. But seek first his kingdom and his righteousness, and all these things will be given to you as well. Therefore do not worry about tomorrow, for tomorrow will worry about itself. Each day has enough trouble of its own." (Matthew 6:28-34)

Jesus apparently wanted his Church to live on the constant edge of dependency on him just as fully as sparrows do. Here he obliterates all connection to the ways of the world. Indeed, his great prayer given to us requires the daily request for bread. In his program, amassing fails to be included. We have progressed(?) from hand to mouth living to shovel to storeroom living.

What irony that the church institutional happens to be the richest of all institutions, tying the church to this world and its systems. Consequently, rather than seek the Kingdom and his righteousness, we tend to seek to operate in the world's system, creating all the financial and political connections demanded to survive and flourish and the anxiety that accompanies.

Everywhere I travel one observation overwhelms and troubles me—the church is a conflicted organization. We have built and organized and administrated until we have lost our peace.

The Kingdom loses its uniqueness as it moves into the cultural arena adopting the culture's standards and systems. Our uniqueness remains with the others-centered, servant-hearted nature of Jesus where we find our life and our peace. Anything else agitates, divides and destroys.

In the childlike realization that our Father loves us immensely and has more than adequate resources, we trust and rest. I think the Father likes to hear our hearts go "Aahhh."

Judgment Deferred

Judging others results from not being truthful about ourselves. An old saying states, "There is a little larceny inside every one of us." God knew it first and stated it more clearly:

"The heart is deceitful above all things, and desperately wicked: who can know it?"
(Jeremiah 17:9)

Knowing the problem of the heart and the difficulty of judging, we in the United States choose twelve people to hear a court case hoping that, collectively, the truth can be discerned. For his own Church, Jesus chooses the following action:

"Do not judge, or you too will be judged. For in the same way you judge others, you will be judged, and with the measure you use, it will be measured to you. Why do you look at the speck of sawdust in your brother's eye and pay no attention to the plank in your own eye? How can you say to your brother, 'Let me take the speck out of your eye,' when all the time there is a plank in your own eye? You hypocrite, first take the plank out of your own eye, and then you will see clearly to remove the speck from your brother's eye." (Matthew 7:1-5)

Judging others distracts us from the focus of winning others. Judging others places us above them rather than as servants to them. Judging others usurps a job that even Jesus refused to take.

The amazing final command in the Scripture above urges us to remove a plank from our own eye. Imagine the pain of having a plank to begin with and then to remove it. Anyone who has had a plank removed from his eye will always be careful with eyes. Anyone who understands the reality of his own guilt will always be careful with others.

Jesus wants his Church to be a group of winners not judgers.

The Return

Jesus said it, we expect it—*"I will come again...."*

"Do not let your hearts be troubled. Trust in God; trust also in me. In my Father's house are many rooms; if it were not so, I would have told you. I am going there to prepare a place for you. And if I go and prepare a place for you, I will come back and take you to be with me that you also may be where I am." (John 14:1-3)

The promise that he would return thrills those who maintain a relationship with Jesus and terrifies those who don't. However, the very promise enlarges life for all who follow him. The teaching of Jesus more than adequately indicates his return and lays the groundwork of expectancy and preparedness. The promise to followers promotes readiness. Notice these statements indicating his return in Matthew 24:

1. False prophets claiming to be Christ
2. Wars and rumors of wars
3. Earthquakes in different (unexpected?) places
4. Famines
5. Persecution
6. Betrayal
7. Defection

8. Gospel preached in the whole world
9. Abomination of desolation (probably desecration of a new temple)

Beginning in verse 27 of Matthew 24, Jesus tells us the dramatic result: *"For as lightning that comes from the east is visible even in the west, so will be the coming of the Son of Man. At that time the sign of the Son of Man will appear in the sky, and all the nations of the earth will mourn. They will see the Son of Man coming on the clouds of the sky, with power and great glory. And he will send his angels with a loud trumpet call, and they will gather his elect from the four winds, from one end of the heavens to the other."*

In the same chapter, Jesus gives further indication of the need for preparedness through the following story/parables:

1. Apathy as in the time of Noah
2. Two men in the field—one taken
3. Two women grinding—one taken
4. House thief with unknowing owner
5. The wise servant who feeds workers at the proper time
6. The five wise and five foolish virgins
7. Man entrusting his servants with talents to use until his return

What are we to do with all this knowledge? Jesus makes the application clear in Matthew 25:13: *"Therefore keep watch, because you do not know the day or the hour."* For those who follow him, this preparedness is no burden and the expectancy is glorious.

So where are we now? All things are ready!

The Church Complete

Perhaps you recall the visual parable in the first chapter of the do-it-yourself furniture I attempted. The result never made the *showpiece* category. However, the furniture, as a reflection of my own ineptness, seemed to be the way the church, as I saw it, looked. Jesus reminded me that the church looked this way because that was the way I put it together, not the way he built it.

Even as these pages have unfolded, seeing the facets of the Church as Jesus, the founder, described, I hear choirs from all the meetings I have ever attended singing of the Church triumphant—leaving layers of goosebumps on my skin. The thought is glorious and encouraging.

Then in one of those almost awake, almost asleep moments, the vision of what his Church looks like struck me. I almost laughed. No great castle or cathedral rose in my mind—no temple or skyscraper, no stone monolith. Instead, there, placed solidly on a rock and firmly stabilized, grew an indescribable house, almost the look of a shack, with lumber obviously gathered from garbage piles. Nothing seemed cut for the house. Along side thick beams that came from nowhere and went nowhere were additions of polished and finished wood. Boards stuck out as if someone lacked a saw. Other boards slapped on the outside with glue or nails appeared to be placed there at odd angles because they fit nowhere else and the builder wanted them to be part of the structure somehow.

Continued observation proved this to be a most unique house. Rather than merely a single unit, the house grew off in different angles, sometimes curving, sometimes making sharp turns. Branches went off at different spots until you could not tell where the house began or ended.

The only unifying feature was the same foundation that extended underneath wherever the house grew. Most of the expanding development appeared to be only one story high with every building connected to the next one; however, I noticed some that had two and three levels. The upper stories looked much more ornate—obviously a different designer and carpenter. Another item shocked me. On either side of the multistory units, someone had taken down parts of the houses that adjoined and built a concrete or brick wall between them so that no one in adjacent houses had any direct touch with the higher houses. The only thing the same about them was the foundation and first story.

Further along, I saw even single story houses with brick walls separating themselves from the other houses. In order to build the walls, they had to destroy part of their own house and sometimes part of the next house. The isolation confused many residents, but still, the same foundation ran under each. A few houses had "Do not disturb" signs hanging on the door. In front of some houses, I saw neighbors in some sort of fight. I could not tell what the fight was about, since each one had adequate housing and yard for themselves.

Some had unusual paint apparently to make sure their houses looked like no other. A few had added uniqueness that seemed designed to irritate the neighbors. In front of one, I saw a moving van taking furniture out of the house. I could not resist asking the occupant what was going on. He didn't hesitate answering, "Well, I don't like it here!"

"Why?"

"I don't like the rules. I have to go outside to smoke and the TV here is horrible."

"Poor reception?"

"No, poor variety. I want some things that seem in short supply here."

"Is the house bad?"

"No, the house is perfect."

"Bad neighbors?"

"No, except hardly anyone is interested in the same things I am."

"Have you been evicted?"

"No, this is my own choice."

"Where are you going?"

"I don't know. Somewhere."

"Where you can be free?"

He paused for a long time and looked at me as if I had asked the worst question possible and then finally answered, "Yes."

Finally, as I got a bird's eye view of the house, I could see it was more like one large, but totally connected city. However, no city hall or police station or stop signs or traffic lights appeared anywhere. I marveled, but instinctively knew where the government came from. Eventually, I came to the end of the houses where single story additions were being built and saw *The Carpenter*. He so enjoyed his work that the sound of the hammer was more like laughter than sharp noise. Finally, he picked up a piece of wood that had never been sheltered. It was weathered, cracked and warped. Never would such a piece be used in a house, but he studied it a bit, turned it in his hands and broke out in total laughter. Then he put a hinge on the end of it and nailed it to a board that stuck out apparently uselessly. Then the carpenter chuckled to himself, "No one will figure out what this is here for. They will only notice it when the wind blows and it clatters, but they won't want to show anyone this side of the house. At least they will know when the wind blows." Then he went on merrily about his building.

I took the opportunity to ask some questions. "Your design is certainly different. How do you convince people they should rent or buy here?"

"Oh! This is not for rent or for sale. This is free housing!"

"Amazing! But still, how do you get people to come here?"

"Well, they have to volunteer for it. Even their children can live here only to a certain time and then they have to volunteer for themselves. No one is ever forced to live here."

"So you are building now for new volunteers. Do you get a lot of them?"

"Oh, yes. Keeps me busy, but I love it."

"But what about the person I saw moving out?" Sadness dropped his face and I saw a tear in his eye.

"I wish it were not so. I never evict anyone and they are perfectly safe here, but they can choose to leave. I respect their choice." His voice trailed off and he looked away. Suddenly a puff of wind sent the hinged, warped piece of wood clattering away. His laughter rescued him from the sadness.

I joined in the laughter and thought that even this house would be beneath what some call a *starter house. Fixer-upper* failed as a description—*bulldozerer* fit better. I wondered at this image in my mind until I heard the whisper: "Gayle, what you built was actually better in the eyes of the world and yourself than mine. You used lumber precut for the purpose.

I salvaged my Church from the junk piles of the world. This is why the world will never understand. Every board I chose I used. Some would support nothing and merely had to be tacked on. But it is mine and it serves my purposes. What else do you think would go with the 'stone that the builders rejected'? *"Have you never read in the Scriptures: 'The stone the builders rejected has become the capstone; the Lord has done this, and it is marvelous in our eyes'?"*

Of course.

Other Books and Resources by Gayle Erwin

The Jesus Style
A unique look at the real Jesus. In 34 languages and 44 printings, this hallmark book remains the book of choice for reading and giving to others.

The Father Style
This book breaks new ground in seeing God the Father through the eyes of Jesus. You will know Him and love Him.

The Spirit Style
The Holy Spirit through the prophecies and life of Jesus. A healing and resolving book.

That Reminds Me of a Story
Forty true and unique stories from the life and observation of Gayle Erwin. It taps the whole range of emotions.

That Reminds Me of Another Story
Gayle shares more of the richness of his life with 60 true and unique stories.

Handbook for Servants
Finally, answers to nagging questions for those who serve.

Video and Audio Tapes and CDs
A rich and extensive group of teachings by Gayle. His delightful insight and humorous approach to Scripture make these very popular to all ages.

Servant Quarters
This magazine/newsletter contains his latest writings, news and reader response. Sent free or read online.

To order or receive a catalog, write:
Servant Quarters, Box 219, Cathedral City, CA 92235
or call toll free 1-888-321-0077

Website: www.servant.org   Email: gayle@servant.org

Gayle Erwin has spent 46 years as a pastor, college teacher, evangelist and magazine creator and editor. He devotes his time now to teaching and writing about the nature of Jesus.